WAKE UP

While You Can

A New, logical, Non-religious

Insight Into

Life after Death

A Logical Spirituality

Sarfraz Zaidi, MD

Wake Up While You Can - A New, Logical, Non-religious Insight Into Life After Death.

First Edition, 2014

ISBN-13: 978-1500434281
ISBN-10: 1500434280
Library of Congress Control Number: 2014915106

CreateSpace Independent Publishing Platform
North Charleston, SC

Printed in the United States of America.

Disclaimer

The information in this book is true and complete to the best of our knowledge. This book is intended only as an informative guide for those on the spiritual journey, who wish to know more about psycho-spiritual-physical health issues.

The information in this book is not intended to replace the advice of a health care provider, spiritual guru or a religious teacher. In no way, we are trying to challenge your religious, cultural or political beliefs.

The author and publisher disclaim any liability for the decisions you make based on the information contained in this book. The information provided herein should not be used during any medical emergency or for the diagnosis and treatment of any medical, psychological or psychiatric condition. In no way is this book intended to replace, countermand or conflict with the advice given to you by your own health care provider, spiritual guru or a religious teacher.

The information contained in this book is general and is offered with no guarantees on the part of the author or publisher. The author and publisher disclaim all liability in connection with the use of this book.

The names and identifying details of people associated with events described in this book have been changed. Any similarity to actual persons is coincidental. These people have given expressed consent to include their experiences in this book.

Any duplication or distribution of information contained herein is strictly prohibited.

Note From The Author

What I describe in this book are my original thoughts, based on my own observations. I write them down as the new ideas pop up in my head. I asked my close friend to proofread the book for any spelling errors. I clearly asked her *not* to make any changes in the sentences or do any editing. So there you have it an, *uncut* version of my original ideas. You may find some repetitions and some grammar issues. I apologize for that.

I do *not* belong to any religious, social or political organization. *I have no mission.* I am *not* trying to impress you, convince you or entertain you. In no way, I am trying to challenge your religious, cultural or political beliefs.

I am *simply* sharing my own observations about life. My tool is simple logic. The book is intended for a reader who uses logic, is open-minded, and is ready for fresh ideas.

.

You don't die only if you are not born!

Sarfraz Zaidi, MD

Contents

Section One

Life after Death

Section Two

Wake Up While You Can

Section Three

Questions and Answers

Chapter 1

Here Is My Story!

I am Sarfraz Zaidi, a medical doctor specializing in Diabetes and Endocrinology. As an endocrinologist, I became fully aware of the complexities of the human brain and how stress can disrupt the normal function of the entire hormonal system in the body. But what, really is stress? How does it affect your body and is it possible to manage stress without medications? For years, I was intrigued by these questions. Not to mention that I was suffering from the stress of daily living myself. Gradually it got worse to the point that I started to have panic attacks.

My Quest For Self Realization

After reading a few books on self-realization, it became clear to me that the root of our stress is *the Self*. "But if I am not my Self, then who am I?" was my question. There was no *satisfactory* answer. Being a medical scientist, I would not accept any answer that did not make sense. Then I decided to use an approach what we physicians use to diagnose tough cases: the process of ruling out. We rule out various causes one by one, until we get to the correct diagnosis. In order to find out who I really am, I decided to see who I am NOT.

My Awakening

With this mindset, one day, as I was walking in our neighborhood park, I suddenly got the answers. A profound wisdom sank in. Things became crystal clear. You could call it an awakening!

Using logic, I realized that I was still myself before I became an accomplished doctor, bought an expensive home in the suburbs and owned a luxury car. I was still myself before I became a husband. I was still myself before I went to medical school, college and high school. And I was still myself before I started elementary school. I was still myself before I started talking, walking, standing, crawling and sitting. And I was still myself when I was born... So, I was myself the REAL me when I was born and everything else, I acquired later on in life. With this realization, a shocking sensation went through my body. Then suddenly, there was relief, as if a huge load was lifted off my shoulders. Then, there was a feeling of inner peace, freedom and joy.

I went to sleep with this mindset. Next morning, I wondered how was I when I was born? Of course, I did not know how I was at birth. Fortunately, I had the opportunity to be in charge of a well-baby nursery in my early career as a doctor and observed about sixty newborns every day. Later, I had the wonderful experience of having my own baby. I reflected back on those experiences. What I realized would change my life forever. Here are my observations:

The REAL Self

As soon as baby's basic physical needs are met (i.e. a full stomach, a clean diaper and a warm blanket), they are *joyful* from within! They *smile* and go to sleep. They have no *past* or *future*. They are *not* worried if mom will be around for the next feed. If they did, they wouldn't be able to go to sleep. They have no *concepts*, no *judging*, no *anger*, no *worries*. That's why they have no problem going to sleep. They are so *vulnerable*, but *fear* remains miles away. There is a total *lack of control,* but *no fear* whatsoever.

Once their stomach is full, they *don't* want any more food. If you were to force more food than they need, they would regurgitate. They eat to satisfy their hunger and that's all. *Wanting more* does not exist and that's why they are so *content*. You could feed them breast milk, cow's milk or formula. To them, it doesn't matter as long as it agrees with their stomach and satisfies their hunger.

They don't say "I don't like your milk, Mom. I like formula better." You would not hear, "Mom, you wrapped me in a pink blanket with butterflies on it. I'm a boy. Therefore, I need a blue blanket with pictures of dinosaurs on it."

They don't think. Why do I say newborn babies don't think? That is because you always think in terms of a language. Right now, you are thinking in terms of English. If you did not know English, these letters would not make any sense to you. Therefore, it is logical to conclude that you need a language to think. Newborns know *no* language. Hence, we can conclude babies don't think. They also have no concepts. Why? That is because concepts arise out of language. No language - no concepts.

Newborns don't like or dislike someone because of their color, religion, nationality or wealth. That's because they have *not* acquired any *concepts* about religion, nationality, history or money. *Concepts* do not exist at all. *Likes and dislikes* do not exist. There are no *preferences or judgments.* No *embarrassment or shame.*

They are joyful just looking around. They truly *live in the Now.* They do it *spontaneously* without making an effort to live in the Now. *No anger, no hate, no wanting more, no prejudices, no fear, just pure joy, contentment and peace.* I like to call it the "REAL Self," the self that you and I and everyone else on the planet are born with.

Wisdom Deepens

Over the next several months, I kept getting more and more wisdom. I would just sit by myself, in the back yard, enjoying Nature. Then some *original* ideas would pop up in my head, I call it wisdom.

11

The Challenge Of A Physical Illness

Then I developed an illness that would last a couple of years. I saw several brilliant doctors, but treatment was not very effective. I am fortunate that the illness happened after I had gotten some wisdom. The previous me would have been miserable, but I walked on this road without any stress. I would simply stay in the NOW and would not experience any psychological stress. Even the physical stress from the illness did not bother me, although my loved ones were getting quite stressed out, because I had lost a significant amount of weight. One day, my wife accurately pointed out, "you look like someone from the concentration camp," as she saw me in the shower.

This illness forced me to cut down my practice hours. I realized even talking would exhaust me. This observation made me realize that the act of talking, in fact, consumes a lot of energy. I would spend more and more time in my bedroom and in the back yard. I would keep myself in the NOW. More and more wisdom kept sinking in. At one point, I became free of the fear of death.

GOD Is REAL

One day, I was having lunch at one restaurant by myself. I was looking at these old trees outside. I was completely in the NOW, sitting quiet and still. There were no thoughts, whatsoever. Suddenly, I was in a different dimension: a dimension of profound stillness, silence and space, although words don't quite describe it. I was awake, fully aware of other people in the restaurant, but they were, as if, in the background. In the foreground was this *immense* stillness, silence and spaciousness. And it was so peaceful.

Then the waiter came and asked me something, which got me out of this dimension. But immense peace was still there in my chest. I suddenly realized that I had just experienced REAL GOD.

Please be advised, I am using the word GOD, simply to communicate with you. In fact, REAL GOD is not a concept. Hence, no word can describe REAL GOD, because every word creates a concept, and REAL GOD is REAL, not a concept.

Since that day in the restaurant, I can get into this dimension any time, by sitting quietly, by myself and keeping my attention completely in the NOW, without any thinking. In this state, I also get some original ideas. I call it wisdom, which I am going to share with you in this book.

Chapter **2**

Conceptual Life After Death

The human mind has created a *conceptual* world: collectively it is the "human world" and individually it is the "virtual I" in every human's head. The virtual "I" does *not* want to die. Therefore, the collective human mind has created the concept of "life after death." In this way, it tries to *escape* the fear of death.

Various religions have created various concepts about life after death. In doing so, religions try to control the behavior of individuals through the powerful tools of reward and punishment, during this life and also the conceptual life after death. For example, there are the concepts of Heaven and Hell. Religion then teaches you how to secure a seat in the most desirable land of *Conceptual* Heaven and how to avoid the most painful fires of *Conceptual* Hell. It basically boils down to the interests of the religious organization in terms of power, control and money, that's all!

While many followers of a religion can see the *conceptual* nature of Heaven and Hell, the *illogical* nature of the religious stories, the *conceptual* nature of God and the *self-interests* of the religious organization, they still continue to follow their religion. Why? In most cases, religion is bestowed upon people by their loving parents as a part of their family values. They do not want to *disrespect*, *disobey* or *disappoint* their loving parents. In addition, most religious activities are in fact social activities. That's why a large number of people continue to participate in these activities. They enjoy the social aspect of these activities. In addition, these activities fulfill their desire to blend in, to belong to some group, to a have purpose in life. Many people are strongly attached to a religion as it fulfills their emotional needs.

Overwhelmed by the emotional attachment to a religion in one way or another, people cannot (or do not) see the selfish, worldly interests of religions. In time, they become parents and download their beloved family values and belief system onto their children and the cycle continues.

Some individuals clearly see religion as a tool to control its believers' behavior. Then, they develop a *negative* attachment towards all what religion stands for: the concept of God, the concept of life and the concept of life after death. They may call themselves atheists or agnostics.

Chapter **3**

Is There Life After Death?

Is there life after death? In order to find the *true* answer, you need to leave behind all you have been told. You need to be free of your attachments, *positive* or *negative*, in order to find answers objectively. Let's embark on this journey together. Personally, I used to be your average religious person. Then I became agnostic. Now I am neither religious nor agnostic.

What Is Life?

Before we can find out if there is life after death, we need to see for ourselves what life really is. Is life your name, your possessions, your career, your relationships, your health, your family, social and cultural values, etc? On the surface, that's what life seems to be, right? People often say, "Life is good. Everything is going for me. I have a great job, my relationships are wonderful and I have great health." Or someone may say, "Oh, my life sucks. I just lost my house, don't have a job and my wife is in the hospital." Some may say, "Life is too short. Enjoy as much as you can." Here are some other sayings about life: "Life is unfair." "Life is a gift." Life is sacred." "Fight for your life." "Pro-life." "Life and death situation."

The Conceptual Life

Use logic and you will realize all of these statements refer to what we can call "conceptual life," which is created by the collective human mind. In this conceptual life, there are concepts about success, failure, wealth, poverty, career, accomplishments, fairness and unfairness, love and hate, beauty and ugliness, sacredness of life, life and death, fight for life, etc.

These concepts get downloaded into a child's mind as he grows up in a society as a part of psycho social conditioning. Concepts give rise to thoughts, which trigger emotions. You feel these emotions and start to believe in concepts to be something real. In fact, a concept is *never* REAL. It is always virtual, conceptual by definition. In this way, all of these concepts about life actually create a conceptual life that we mistakenly believe in as life.

REAL Life

In contrast there is REAL Life, which flows through every life form. This life is neither short, nor long, neither good nor bad, neither sacred nor sinful. Life simply is! It never ends. A life form comes to an end, but *not* life itself. The opposite of death is birth, not life. Actually life has *no* opposite.

REAL Life is not a concept. Hence, it is beyond the comprehension of the conditioned human mind. But the human mind wants to interpret it, as it wants to do with everything. Therefore, it has created the concepts of cell, DNA, RNA, molecule, atom, subatomic particles, photons, Quantum, etc. The list of these concepts about life continues to grow, but here is a simple fact. Life is not a concept. Therefore, any concept, philosophy or knowledge about life keeps you away from the Reality of life. It is such an irony, but the human mind does not understand it.

Here are a couple of examples to illustrate these points:

With all of the immense understanding about the ultra-microscopic structure of life forms, the human mind cannot produce a living form from scratch. It can't even produce simple parts of a life form, such as a feather, a leaf, or even a flower.

During organ transplantation, a surgeon takes an organ, let's say a heart from a dead body, where it had stopped working. When put it in a body with *life*, it starts to function again.

REALITY is always what you can sense with your senses. REAL life is flowing through you and you can sense it, right now. Pause from reading this book. Take your attention into your chest, pay attention to every breath. After a little while, you will sense a vibrant energy flowing throughout your body. This is REAL life energy. It is always there, in your body. But you don't sense it, because your attention is consumed by the busy mind.

Chapter 4

Conceptual Soul Versus Real Soul

The human mind has also created a concept of Soul. Various religions and philosophies have created various concepts of Soul, and what happens to it after death.

In contrast to the conceptual Soul, there is a Real entity residing in every living being. It is REAL. Therefore, I like to call the REAL Self, the self that you, and I, and every life form is born with. Actually no word can precisely describe it. Why? Because it is REAL and every word is a concept. I am using this term simply to communicate with you.

While we can never conceptualize or interpret what REAL Self is, we can clearly be aware of it. But how? You can be aware of it right now. It is your REAL Self that sees, hears, smells, tastes, and touches. So, it is your REAL Self that is seeing the pages in this book at this moment.

Your REAL Self utilizes eyes and brain to see, ears and brain to hear, nose and brain to smell, tongue and brain to taste, skin and brain to touch, legs and brain to walk, hands and brain to climb etc.

It is your REAL self that experiences emotions. Sometimes you feel sad, sometimes you feel happy, sometimes you feel bored, sometimes you feel excited, sometimes you feel annoyed and irritated, sometimes you feel angry, sometimes you feel hateful, sometimes you feel loving and compassionate, sometimes you feel guilty, sometimes you feel anxiety, sometimes you feel jealous etc. Who feels these emotions? Your REAL Self.

REAL Self is present throughout your body: It lives inside the building of your body. Its main "living room" is inside your chest. That's why you feel emotions in your chest: sometimes a knot, sometimes a raw wound, sometimes elation, etc.

You can see another person's emotions in their eyes. You can see excitement, sadness, happiness, anger, guilt, worries, in another person's eyes. Did you ever wonder why you see another person's emotions in their eyes? It is because the Real Self sees through the eyes. And it is the REAL self that experiences emotions. So if the REAL self is sad, you see that in the eyes. If the REAL self is happy, you see that in the eyes. If the REAL self is mad, you see that in the eyes. If the REAL self is loving, you see that in the eyes. If the REAL self is hateful, you see that in the eyes, etc. A person may fake their emotions, as actors do. But still, it is their REAL Self that experiences those emotions.

Besides emotions, REAL Self also lives in another dimension, but only rarely. You may have experienced a moment or two in your life, when your thoughts and emotions come to a *complete* standstill for a few seconds. You experience something out there as well in your chest, which is so peaceful. By the way, it is not love, happiness or excitement, which are all emotions. This dimension, we can call the REAL NOW, the dimension of REAL GOD.

Newborn babies live in this dimension spontaneously. Since my awakening, I can get in this dimension by freeing myself from thoughts and emotions. For the sake of communication, I will try to describe it, although no words can accurately describe it. I feel an immense peace, space, silence and stillness inside my chest and everywhere, as far as I can see. This is REAL God.

You too can experience REAL GOD right now. Please put this book down. Go outside. Sit down and be still. Pay attention to: what you see, what you hear, smell, taste and touch. While you see, do not make any interpretations. Just see. Also, be aware of the space in which every object is. It is helpful to look at a plant and be aware of the space all around and inside the tree. Do it for a few minutes. Now, also become aware of the silence, which is everywhere. Sounds come out of it and go back into it. Listen to some sound that has no meaning, such a bird chirping. While listening to sound, also become aware of the silence in the background. Then also become aware of the stillness. All movements take place in the sea of stillness. Move your hand slowly back and forth, while paying attention to the movement, as well as its background. In this way, you become aware of stillness.

Once you are fully aware of Space, Silence and Stillness, be aware of the *inside* of your chest. Can you sense space, silence, stillness and an immense peace? This is what I feel. Don't get frustrated if you don't sense it initially. Also be advised that you will also feel an immense *energy* running throughout your body. This is the life energy. In fact, this is quite easy to feel, but to feel space, silence, stillness and peace, you need to be fully free of the grip of the *human* world, which I will elaborate later in this book.

REAL Self can be either lost in the emotions and the busy mind *or* it can be in touch with space, silence, stillness inside you and all around you, which is the REAL GOD. In touch with REAL GOD, it experiences immense peace: the peace of GOD, which is not an emotion.

With few exceptions, the REAL Self of all mankind stays lost in the emotions and the busy mind. In this way, it stays out of touch with the Reality of GOD.

<u>REAL Self is there even in the absence of eyes, ears, nose, tongue and skin</u>. For example, when you dream, you don't use eyes, ears, nose, tongue or skin. Who watches the dream?

It's your REAL Self. In the same way, your REAL Self is there even after the death of your eyes, ears, nose, tongue, skin and the rest of the body. Therefore, it is logical to conclude there is REAL life after death.

Chapter 5

REAL Life After Death

REAL life after death is in the form of your REAL Self, which is devoid of a physical body. Therefore, we need to look at the REAL Self to have a *glimpse* about life after death.

As we just observed, it is your REAL Self that sees, hears, smells, tastes and touches. It is the REAL Self that sees the dreams at night. Now imagine you are having a nightmare. In fact, it is your REAL Self that is *watching* the bad dream and *experiencing* the bad emotion: fear, anger, hate etc. How does a nightmare come to end? When you wake up. You or rather your REAL Self realizes that the dream was not real. In other words, your REAL Self has to be able to *see* through the eyes as well as use *common sense* to be free of the grip of the nightmare.

REAL Hell And Heaven

Now what happens if you die while watching the nightmare? After death, your REAL Self can neither see through the eyes *nor* can it use common sense. Therefore, your REAL Self would *continue* to experience the bad emotions created by the nightmare. Perhaps, this is what REAL hell is. On the other hand, you may die while you are watching a happy dream. Then your Real Self will *continue* to experience the happy emotions of the dream. Perhaps, this is what REAL heaven is.

Now consider this. You not only experience emotions during dreams, but you almost continuously experience emotions while you are awake. Each and every emotion leaves an *imprint* on your REAL Self. After death, your REAL S elf continues to experience these emotions. It suffers emotional pains due to bad emotions. In this life span, you may use various <u>escapes</u> to *cope* with your emotional pains, such as drugs, alcohol, entertainment, vacationing, partying, work etc. In the life after death, you cannot run to these escapes. Then you suffer from these painful emotions with nowhere to run to. On the other hand, REAL Self also experience happiness due to good emotions. In other words, it lives in REAL hell or REAL heaven, depending upon the type of emotions it experiences.

An individual usually has layers of emotions, some bad emotions and some good emotions, piled on each other. After death, Your REAL Self re-experiences all of these emotional imprints, layer by layer. Therefore, it is logical to conclude that the REAL Self lives in REAL hell when it is re-experiencing bad emotions. And it lives in REAL heaven as it re-experiences good emotions. REAL hell and REAL heaven are emotional states of the REAL Self and *not* some walled communities.

Eternal Peace / Peace Of REAL GOD

When a REAL Self is *free* of all of the emotional burden, it will be neither in REAL hell nor in REAL heaven. You can experience this *state* right now. Shift your attention from your busy mind to the REAL NOW in front of your eyes, which is REAL GOD as I described earlier. What I experience in this state: sheer peace: the peace of REAL GOD.

Therefore, when a REAL Self lives in the NOW-in touch with REAL GOD, free of all thoughts and associated emotions, it experiences an inner peace, which is different from love, hate, happiness, sadness or any other emotions. After death, such a REAL Self continues to experience this inner peace. We can call it Eternal Peace or Peace Of REAL GOD.

Chapter **6**

How Emotions Affect Our Body

Emotions are like a storm in your body, which affects your entire physical body (including brain), life energy and REAL Self. In this way, emotions affect your physical, psychological, and spiritual health.

In scientific terms, emotions affect your nervous system, immune system and endocrine system. These *three* systems control the function of every organ in the body including brain, nerves, heart, blood vessels, stomach, intestines, lungs, skin, muscles, adrenal glands, testis, and ovaries.

Here are a few examples:

By affecting your nervous system, your emotions can cause anxiety, depression, bipolar affective disorder, stress eating, psychosis, stomach hyperacidity, irritable bowel syndrome, tense muscles, headaches etc. Emotions can wreak havoc on the immune system, predisposing you to infections, cancer and autoimmune diseases. By affecting your endocrine system, emotions can lead to lack of menses, adrenal fatigue, lack of puberty, lack of growth, low testosterone etc. By affecting your nervous and endocrine systems, emotions can set up the stage for high blood pressure, heart attack, stroke and diabetes. For more details on this, please refer to my book, "Stress Cure Now."

In addition, emotions leave deep *imprints* on your REAL Self, the spirit, the soul. That's why you feel emotions in your *chest*, the main housing place of the REAL Self. In this way, the REAL Self gets *tarnished* with emotional memories: good as well as bad memories. Emotions associated with bad memories are *anger*, *hate*, *guilt*, *jealousy*, *bitterness* and *fear*. How about good memories? In addition to the so-called good emotions such as *love* and *happiness*, good memories can also create sad emotions in the form of "missing." To learn more about memories, please refer to my book, "Stress Cure Now."

Now, what happens when someone dies? The REAL Self is released back into the vastness of space, stillness and silence. However, it carries the emotional imprints with it, once it leaves a physical body. What happens next depends upon the type of the imprints that the REAL Self is *tarnished* with.

Chapter 7

Rebirth

If the REAL Self is *positively* attached to the concept of birth and *negatively* attached to the concept of death, as is the case with most individuals, it tries to be reborn. Therefore, it enters any newly forming physical body, and carries all of the emotional burden with it. Then during the next lifespan, it adds some more emotional burden. In this way, it continues to re-live through a never-ending series of life spans. With each life span, the emotional burden gets heavier and heavier. In some religions, it is called reincarnation. These days, many people consider it highly desirable, because they think they can *beat* death in this way and live forever. In fact, they continue to add to the pile of emotional burden, with each successive life span.

What Type of a New Life Form?

What type of new life form a *tarnished* REAL Self will take simply follows the <u>rule of Probability</u>. At any given moment, an incredibly huge number of life forms are being born. For example, just consider how many ants, bees and mosquitoes there are. Therefore, the tarnished REAL Self can be *reborn* as any one of the life forms: a bird, an animal, an insect, a fish, a reptile, a human, etc. In this way, you have an incredibly low probability to be reborn as a human.

Any Advantage of Being Born Human?

Is there any true advantage of being born as a human, as compared to a fish, a reptile, an insect or an animal ? In fact there is. Only humans have the most evolved brain. With that they have developed what we can call simple logic. We don't go to school to learn it.

In my observation, animals don't have this simple logic. For example, a horse does not know how powerful he is. If he knew, he wouldn't continue to suffer the pains of the metallic piece that humans put in his mouth to keep him under control. If chickens knew there is plenty of food for everyone, they would not be chasing after each other for that one piece of bread, etc.

It is this simple logic that can *liberate* you from the heavy burden of emotions, as I will discuss later in the book. Therefore, it is only as a human being that you have the <u>chance</u> to cleanse your *tarnished* REAL Self and *end* the cycle of rebirths. Therefore, <u>wake up while you can</u>.

Chapter 8

Emotional Entities

Some *tarnished* REAL Self may become so attached to its body and/or its role that it *wants* to get back into its <u>own</u> dead body. It may want to carry on some *unfinished* business, duty, responsibility or a mission. But it can't get back into its own dead body, obviously. Then it hangs around as an <u>entity</u> without a body, experiencing emotional trauma over and over again.

<u>Here are some examples:</u>

- A soldier may want to continue to be a soldier and continue to kill his enemy, but now he is dead. So he wants to get back into his dead body and carry on killing his enemy. But he can't get back in his own dead body. Consequently, he hangs around as an entity, suffering from hateful emotions.
- A person may be strongly attached to her physical appearance, and wants to continue to live in that body. But now the body is dead and she can't live in it any longer. Consequently, she hangs around as an entity, suffering from the sad emotion of *missing* her beautiful body.
- A person may want to take revenge of his unfair death. But he can't get back in his dead body. Now he lives an entity and suffers from *bitterness* and *hate*.
- A person may be strongly attached to his house and want to continue to live in that house. So he hangs around as an entity, living in that house. But feels *angry*

and *fearful* at the new owners of the house, who he thinks are the intruders.

- A person may be strongly attached to his wife, child, friend or a pet. After death, he wants to continue to play his role, but can't. So he lives as an entity suffering from guilt, jealousy and the sad emotion of missing.

- A person may be strongly attached to a political, religious or a social party. As a dead person, he wants to carry on his mission, but can't. Now he hangs around as an entity suffering from fear, anger and jealousy.

- A person may be strongly attached to money or other possessions such as a car, jewelry, clothes. But she can't get back in her dead body to continue to enjoy her possessions. Consequently, she lives as an entity and suffer from a never-ending sadness.

- A person may be strongly attached to entertainment in the form of movies, music, video games etc, but now she can't. After death, she can't access any of her entertainments, then she may live as an entity, bored, irritated and sad.

The Fate of the Emotional Entities

During a lifetime, a person keeps piling on emotional memories, one on top of another, in chronological order, the latest one being on top.

What emotional memory you have at the time of death strongly affects your fate soon after death. Here are few examples:

You may have a strong emotional attachment to a house for one reason or another, at the time of your death. After death, you will end up as an emotional entity as your tarnished REAL Self cannot get back into your own body - something it really wants. Consequently, you will hang around your house as an emotional entity, especially if your spouse or children live in, your other positive attachments. If your spouse or children

32

decide to leave the house and move into some other house, your attachment to the house may also wean off, especially if it was due to attachment to your family members. Then, you can be free to move on, according to what is the next emotional *stain* on your REAL Self. It may be your attachment to birth. Then you will be reborn.

On the other hand, your attachment to your house may be extremely strong. Then you will hang around as an emotional entity as long that house is there. Only after the house is demolished, you will be able to move on, according to the next emotional stain on your REAL self.

You may be strongly attached to your spouse at the time of your death. Then, you will hang around as an emotional entity, missing her/him a lot. Then, one day your spouse is dead. Then, you can move on, according to what is next emotional stain on your REAL Self. Perhaps this explains why couples who strongly love each other, die within a short period of the death of the other spouse.

You may be strongly attached to your little children at the time of your death. Then, you will hang around as an emotional entity until your children are grown ups. Then, you can move on, according to what is next emotional stain on your REAL Self.

You may be suffering from some chronic illness or disability towards the end of your life span. Consequently, you may develop a negative attachment towards your body. After death, you will hang around as an emotional entity for a while. At some point, your REAL Self will get down to the next emotional attachment, which may be a strong attachment to political/social/religious systems. Then, your emotional entity will stay in competition, on a mission. Consequently, it will continue to re-experience the emotions you did when you were in competition and on a mission such as frustration, jealousy, and restlessness.

Suicide

Suicide is an extreme form of "negative attachment" to your own body. Obviously, you have extreme *negative* emotions at the time of your death. Then, you hang around as an emotional entity: strong *negative* emotions constantly *torturing* it. For a while, there is no ending, as it does *not* even want to get back into a new physical body due to its strong negative attachment to body at the time of death. After some time, it may move on to the next emotional stain, which may be depression. So it will suffer from sadness for a while. The next emotional layer may be guilt. So it suffers from guilt for a while, etc.

The Composition Of The Emotional Entity

If you want to find out how you will be as an emotional entity after-death, simply observe how you are now, in this life span. If you are an angry person now, you will be an angry emotional entity. If you are fearful now, you will be a fearful emotional entity after death. If you are a happy person, you will be a happy emotional entity.

However, most people have many layers of emotions in their lifespan. Therefore, they will probably experience all of these emotions after death as an emotional entity: from jealousy to anger to fear to boredom to sadness to happiness, etc. They also carry these emotions into their next life span when they are reborn.

Why Emotional Entities Cannot Find Eternal Peace/
Peace of REAL GOD

If you stay out of touch with NOW-REAL GOD, while you are alive, you continue to stay away from REAL GOD after you die. Consequently, you continue to stay in the grip of your emotions in this life and in the life after death. Even though REAL GOD is all around you, in this life and in the life after death. Therefore, you do not find eternal peace in this life or in the life after death.

Emotional Entities Can Perch On you

Sometimes these entities may *perch* on a living person, if their desire to live in a body is very strong. Then, they may influence the living body and may cause some physical or emotional illness to that person.

These emotional entities try to find a living person with similar emotional characteristics as their own. For example, a *dead* hateful person may perch on the *living* body of another hateful person and make him even more hateful. A *dead* greedy person may perch on the *living* body of another greedy person and make him even greedier. A *dead* loving person may perch on the *living* body of another loving person and make him more loving and sad due to missing. A *dead* fearful person may perch on the living body of another fearful person and make her more fearful. Perhaps this partially explains why the human world continues to experience more and more emotional drama, with the passage of time.

Emotional entities not only affect your psychological and mental health, but can also affect your physical health. For example, an angry emotional entity can make you even angrier. A lot of anger raises your blood pressure and blood sugar, and can cause you to have a heart attack, stroke and dementia. A fearful emotional entity can make you more fearful. A lot of fear causes you to suffer from an autoimmune disorder such as asthma, eczema, colitis, Gluten sensitivity, Irritable Bowel Syndrome, Graves' disease, Hashimoto's thyroiditis, Type 1 diabetes, lupus, etc.

Many spiritual/religious leaders create the concept of "ghosts and evil spirits." They then take advantage of *naive* people and promise to get rid of the evil spirits through their tricks in exchange for a large sum of money. Which obviously does not work. Even if you are rid of one emotional entity, you will end up attracting another emotional entity, sooner or later. It is only when you stop sending emotional signals that you are free of attacks by emotional entities.

Only when a person truly wakes up during his lifetime, does he not have any emotional attachments: No attachment to money, fame, power, etc. Therefore, any spiritual guru/teacher who seeks fame, power, money, etc is himself really *not* free of emotions. How can he get rid of your emotional entities? Only a truly awakened person, free of all attachments, frees himself of the emotions from this life and any past lives. None of the "entities" can perch on such a person because they have *nothing* in common. A truly enlightened person has *no* emotional signals, whatsoever.

Therefore, the only way you are not a landing ground for a floating "emotional entity" is to get rid of your own emotions, through awakening, *not* by suppressing them, as I will discuss later in the book. Perhaps, now you understand why you need to wake up while you can.

Chapter **9**

Emotional Entities Influence Little Babies' Health And Behavior

The REAL Self continues to add more and more emotional burden during each lifespan as a human. Consequently, there are a lot of entities floating around, heavily loaded with emotional burden. When such an emotional entity is reborn as a human, that baby starts to exhibit signs of emotional distress early in life.

Emotions affect every system in the body, such as the respiratory system, gastrointestinal system, immune system, neurological system etc. A heavy emotional entity in a baby may be responsible for symptoms such as colic, asthma like episodes, emotional fits, etc. In addition, there may be medical reasons for these symptoms. But in the absence of an identifiable cause for these symptoms, a heavily emotion-laden entity is a likely culprit.

What type of emotional entity gets into a newly forming fetus depends upon the emotional make-up of the parents and other people living close to the mother during early pregnancy such as siblings and grandparents. For example, if a parent or any other person in the household is very fearful and anxious, the fetus is likely to get an emotional entity, which is loaded with the emotion of fear. In the same way, an angry self-righteous parent may attract an angry emotional entity for their baby. On the other hand, a happy parent will likely attract a happy emotional entity for their baby.

Sometimes both parents have similar emotional make-up. For example, both parents may be happy. They will likely attract a happy emotional entity for their baby. Or both may be anxious then they will likely attract an anxious emotional entity for their baby.

Often, parents have different personalities. One may be a happy, easy-going person and the other may be anxious or angry. Now, each parent will attract an emotional entity similar to his or her emotional make-up. Which emotional entity gets into the developing fetus is a matter of chance. This phenomenon explains why children in the same family have such a variation in their personalities. Even twins may have very dissimilar personalities, right from very early age: one may be happy, easy-going while the other may be cautious, and fearful.

Even the same parent may be happy during one pregnancy and unhappy during another pregnancy. The type of emotional entity he/she attracts will depend upon his/her mood during early pregnancy. This phenomenon may explain why babies born out of rape often have such difficult behavior right from early childhood.

In addition, a baby's behavior is shaped according to the type of emotional environment a baby grows up in. Even an angry emotional entity can acquire a lot of love if that love, is provided by the parents. In the same way, even a loving emotional entity can add a lot of hate and anger if she grows up in household full of hate and anger.

In summary, a person's personality is a combination of the type of emotional entity that gets in that baby and later, what type of emotional household, she grows up in.

Chapter 10

Dreams Can Be a Window Into Life After Death

Here are my observations about dreams. There are two types of dreams:

1. Memory-Replay Dreams

Common types of dreams are basically a *replay* of your emotional memories in a *random* manner. The underlying thread is an emotion. Then a number of memories carrying this emotion get pulled together in a random fashion. A random compilation of these memories constitutes your dream. Your REAL Self experiences this emotion while watching the dream.

Emotional memories are based on your past experiences. In addition, you also have emotional memories in the form of virtual experiences such as being a dedicated fan of a celebrity without ever meeting the celebrity. Or getting emotionally involved in a movie or a TV show, etc. Your REAL Self (soul) also carries emotional memories from its previous lives. In this way, you have a huge pile of emotional memories, which serve as building blocks for your dreams.

Example:

The underlying emotion may be fear. A number of emotional memories, each with fear as a part of it, get scrambled into a dream. You experience fear while watching your dream. This is what we call a nightmare. The next morning, you may realize some of the components of the dream are true, but details are not accurate.

Example:

The underlying emotion may be excitement. A number of emotional memories, each with excitement as a part of it, get randomly organized into a dream. You feel excitement while watching the dream. The next morning, you may remember the details of your dream, some of which make sense and others don't.

Example:

The underlying emotion may be anger. A number of emotional memories, each with anger as a part of it, get randomly put together as a dream. You get angry while watching the dream. This is what we call a nightmare. The next morning, you may remember the details of your dream, some of which make sense and others which don't.

2. New-Experience Dreams

These types of dreams are rare. In these dreams you have a direct new experience, rather than a replay of emotional memories. Usually, a dead emotional entity shows up in your dream. This emotional entity is *usually*, but not always, your loved one who has recently passed away. You are fully aware that it is a dead person, although it looks just like a living person.

These dreams are different from the usual Memory-Replay dreams in which you may re-experience your memories of that dead person. In Memory-Replay dreams, you are *not* aware that person is dead. For example, you may re-experience emotional memories from your childhood of your deceased father, as if they are happening now.

40

In a New-Experience dream, the dead emotional entity gets connected to your REAL Self through your brain, which contains the stored images of that person. That's why you see that emotional entity in a form that you are familiar with. Often, the common *glue* is the strong emotion between you and the deceased person.

Here are few real examples:

1. My mother and I were closely emotionally attached. She had a stroke in middle age that affected her walking, so that she lived the last several years of her life in a wheelchair. During this time, I brought her to my house and took care of her. That's when we developed a special bond. The stroke did not affect her mental functioning. She stayed mentally sharp until her death. Her biggest wish was to be able to walk again.

Her death was a big shock for all of the family. For several weeks, I missed her tremendously. I would talk to my brother in Canada a lot about our mutual grief. He was also very close to her, as she had lived with him for a while on her way to the U.S. My brother is a non-religious, family-loving person, and an engineer by profession.

A few weeks after her death, my mother appeared in my brother's dream. She was sitting next to her grave and was crying. My brother was fully aware that she was dead.

My emotional pain of missing my mother subsided with the passage of time. Several months later, she suddenly appeared in my dream one night. I was fully aware that she was dead. She appeared how she used to look when she was young. She walked without any problem and appeared very happy. She told me she was living on some other planet with some guy. She talked to me a lot, most of which I do not remember. However, I remember that she proudly showed me their shopping area. Finally, I vividly remember, she told someone, "It's time to take him back to earth, before it gets dark or some bad spirits may cause trouble with his journey."

This was the first and so far the only time that I saw her in my dream as a dead person. It has been more than 15 years since she passed away.

This is what I make of these two dreams:

Soon after her death, my mother's emotional entity missed us a lot, while we were also missing her. She experienced a lot of sad emotions of missing us. That's why she appeared sad in my brother's dream.

With the passage of time, we stopped missing her. At some point, this led her to stop missing us, too. Then, her emotional entity moved on to be reborn somewhere as a healthy person, who was able to walk without any problems.

2. My brother was in his teens when he dreamt one night that someone died in our next door neighbor's house. In his dream, he did not see the person, but saw a coffin being carried out of their house. The next morning, we heard that an old man had died that night in that very house. We had recently moved into our own house and had not met our neighbors yet.

My Thoughts About This Dream

The old man's soul appeared in my brother's dream, soon after it left its own body. As my brother's brain did not have any image of this person, it pulled out a symbol of death in the form of a coffin. Had my brother known this person, then his brain would have kept an image of that person and that image would have appeared in the dream.

3. Meet Pardeep, a non-religious person, an engineer by profession and a devoted family man.

One day, Pardeep's wife died after a long medical illness. They had been married for a long time and had two grown children. His wife was very attached to her children, as well as possessive about her husband. She was a religious person and believed in reincarnation. She was a physician by profession.

Pardeep missed her a lot. Over the next couple of years, he saw her in his dream two times. He was fully aware that she was dead. She was in their bedroom, having their usual household chat. Mostly, she was very concerned about the wellbeing of her children.

With the passage of time, he stopped missing her. At some point, he started dating another woman. Since then, she stopped appearing in his dreams.

My thoughts about this dream:

Her emotional entity continued to carry the emotion of love for her husband and children. Once Pardeep stopped missing her and started to date, her emotional entity moved on, perhaps to get reborn.

4. Meet Lisa, a young college graduate, pursuing her career in Hollywood as a visual effect editor. Lisa is non-religious, but a spiritual person.

Lisa saw her paternal grandmother in her dream one night. She was fully aware that her grandmother was dead. Her grandmother told her, "I can visit you in your dreams."

Her grandmother was a loving, caring person and held high morals. She was married to an abusive husband, who once threatened to kill her at gunpoint. At that juncture, she divorced him. Throughout her life, she attended church regularly.

Several years later, Lisa saw her grandmother again. This time, Lisa was not asleep, but in a trance-like state. The message that Lisa remembered was, "Follow your instincts and you will be safe."

At that time, Lisa had just met a man at a public library in Hollywood. He was nice looking, well dressed and charming. They exchanged phone numbers and made plans to go on a date. When he called her to set up a time for their first date, he seemed to be a different person and made some bizarre sexual comments and eventually offered her a large amount of money just to wear a pair of pantyhose. Lisa was freaked out by the phone call and told him never to call her again. She was bothered the most that he had totally "gone under her radar." She thought she was good judge of character, but she was completely wrong about him.

A couple of years later, Lisa was shocked to see the same man on the news. He was a serial killer who stalked women in Los Angeles for several years. He would pick up girls, often prostitutes, to torture and kill. Often, he would offer them a large amount of money for some easy task. He called some of his victims from the public library where Lisa met him. Finally, Lisa realized why her grandmother had appeared to her. She came to warn her of a danger that had entered her life.

My thoughts about this dream:

Grandmother's emotional entity was still hanging around many years after her death. She was very sensitive to any abusive person. As a loving, caring grandmother, she was very protective of her grandchild. She could sense the bad emotions in the serial killer, who had successfully hid those emotions from the radar of Lisa's judgment.

5. Meet Dorothy, a non-religious person, a retired English teacher by profession. Here is her experience about an after-death-visitation, in her own words.

During my late 20's into my late 30's I lived next door to a young gay man that became a very close friend. We could and would talk about any and everything, and over the course of the nine years he was my next door neighbor, I came to value him as my best friend.

When I moved to acreage in the country, about an hour's drive away, we still remained close. He and other friends spent many a weekend with me helping me get my old country home repainted, landscaped, and generally "livable."

Being a gay man, he had a great sense of style and was really excited to help me "decorate" my country place. There was one thing in my house his design sensibilities could not accept, however, and he never missed the opportunity to tell me about it every time he came to visit me. It was my "desk," which was really just an old French Door set up on two old 10 gallon aquarium stands. I had a piece of glass that fit perfectly over the top of it, but it only covered about 2/3 of the door. I had another piece of glass cut for it to cover the remaining 1/3 of the door. In each of the 16 panes of the French Door, I had placed pictures and other small knick-knacks which remained dust free, except for the panes under the seam where the two pieces of cover glass met. It drove him crazy that I did not just buy one single piece of glass to cover the entire door.

About a year after I moved to the country, he was diagnosed with AIDS, which at that time (early 80's) was a death sentence. We remained close and he continued to come to visit me often. Our conversations were often about death, the possibility of life after death, and other heavy, esoteric topics. One day he told me that if I ever saw my rocking chair rocking away with no one in it, that I shouldn't be scared because it would be his spirit coming to visit me after his body died. He moved far away to be cared for by his family the last year of his life. He died 3 and a half years after his initial diagnosis.

I missed him and thought of him often. One night, about 6 years after his death, I woke up from sleep because I clearly heard him call my name. I must have been dreaming, but it was so loud and unmistakably his voice, I sat up in bed and tried to recall what I had been dreaming, to no avail.

As I sat there in bed, I heard a low groaning sound. I can't really describe the sound, but it became louder and I realized (1) I was **not** dreaming and (2) it was coming from the spare bedroom. I swung my legs over the side of my bed, about to get up and go down the 10 foot hall way connecting my bedroom to the spare bedroom. Before I got off the bed, as I stared down the hallway, I saw the book laden shelves located above my "French Door desk" pull away from the wall and come crashing down. I was seated on my bed as I watched every book falling down in slow motion onto the glass and shattering it into pieces. I remember thinking my computer and printer would be destroyed as I watched the books and shelves come crashing down.

It all probably happened in less than 30 seconds, but time seemed like it had slowed down. I don't know how long I sat in shock on the edge of my bed before getting up and going into the spare bedroom to survey the damage.

Amazingly, the computer and printer were not damaged. The only thing destroyed was the glass on top of my "French Door desk"....the two pieces of glass that so offended my deceased gay friend's design sense!

I immediately felt goose bumps and then a warm, happy feeling came over me. I knew my friend's spirit had awakened me so I could see the event that would result in my replacing the two broken pieces of glass with what he always maintained should cover the desk; one piece of glass to cover the entire French Door. I remember laughing through my tears and "talking" to him out loud saying, "OK, Peter, now I'm finally going to have this fixed the way you always said it should be."

Did he cause the shelves to come crashing down? Did he know it would happen on this particular night and wait until then to awaken/contact me? I don't know, but what I do know in every fiber of my mortal heart & soul is that he, his soul, his spirit, his "energy" spark of life that lives on beyond mortal death, woke me up so I could witness the event. I have no doubt it was him *and now I have no doubt that something lives on after mortal death.*

    It is pretty clear to me that there is life after death. Upon death of the body, the REAL Self (soul) leaves the body and exists out there in the vastness. It can get connected to a living person during sleep. Usually, it visits those living persons that it was strongly emotionally attached to. The REAL Self (soul) connects through the brain of the living person, igniting an image of the dead person that is stored in the brain of the living person. That's why the dead person appears in our dreams as we remember them when they were alive.

Chapter 11

Emotional Entities Can Get In Touch With You While You Are Awake

Meet Susan, a compassionate, religious, spiritual person.

When she was a child, she woke up one night at 3 am with a sense of "choking." Then, she felt an invisible cloud of energy moving through her house, leaving through a window towards the mountains. The next morning, she learned that during the night, her aunt had committed suicide by keeping her car running in a closed garage. Her dead body had marks of her hands on her neck.

About a year earlier, Susan and her aunt talked about death and life after death. They promised to each other that whoever died first would come back, if possible, to let the other person know if there was life after death.

Eight months after her aunt's death, Susan saw her aunt sitting in front of her grandmother's house, across from Susan's house. Her aunt wore a black dress. It is interesting to note that Susan's mother had made sure that all of her children wore black dresses in memory of their aunt. Susan was getting sick and tired of wearing black dresses all the time.

Moments later, Susan felt an invisible cloud of energy flowing through her house, then leaving through a window towards the mountains. The next morning, Susan found out that her dad had passed away the night before, around the same time (according to Coroner's report) when she felt the invisible cloud of energy in her house.

Meet Lisa again. She was very attached to her maternal grandmother, who was known to be a flamboyant person. "Hurricane" was her nick-name.

Several years after her grandmother's death, Lisa was in a massage parlor. As she laid on the massage table with her face looking down, her masseuse left to get something from another room. At that moment, Lisa thought of her grandmother, who had arranged for her first massage when she visited her in Austria as a youth. Suddenly, Lisa felt her grandmother's presence. Then, she felt a heavy blow to her backside that knocked the wind out of her. In a moment, it was all over. During this time the masseuse was not in the room. Lisa was by herself. There is no question in Lisa's mind that it was her grandmother who gave her a blow to her back, laughing and leaving instantaneously, just like a "Hurricane."

Lisa had another incredible experience in her early years. She grew up in Texas in a family of five. Each year, they spent their summer vacation on their family ranch, which had once been a slave plantation. Although the grand plantation home had long ago burned down in a fire, the Overseer's house was still in good condition and was used by the family for their stays. The Overseer's house as well as the plantation house were built by the slaves. Scattered around the ranch were numerous crumbling brick ruins from slave times, including a sugar mill and blacksmith's shop, Also at the ranch, in a remote location, there was a cemetery for the slaves.

When she was 14, Lisa had an amazing experience. Lisa and her sister were able to drive their old truck across pastures that were usually inaccessible. The weeds and brambles had recently been shredded and a drought had kept the marshy areas dry. They decided to see if they could find the old cemetery that they had heard about. They did find it, but Lisa soon felt strange. She felt the presence of many spirits. She said it felt like they all knew her and were curious to see her. She didn't feel threatened by them, but they hovered near her and seemed to follow her around until she neared the perimeter of the ranch where they just seemed to evaporate. At the time, she did not tell anyone what she experienced. She felt like she had lost her mind and was very shaken by the whole experience. Many years later, one of her friends hypnotized her just for fun. Lisa didn't believe she could be hypnotized. However, she was able to "go under." Under hypnosis, Lisa saw herself as a mulatto women dancing in the living room of the Overseer's house on the ranch. She saw everything from the point of view of the mulatto woman as she danced around the room with joy and abandonment. Lisa said she knew it was during slave times and she was one of the slaves. As she came out of hypnosis, she felt extreme generalized itching for a while.

Lisa believes that she is the reincarnated spirit of the mulatto woman on the ranch that she saw under hypnosis. That's why those spirits in the cemetery came to greet her, as one of their own.

In conclusion, emotional entities (souls) can get in touch with you even when you are awake.

Chapter **12**

Near-Death Experiences

Near-Death experiences gives us a clue into life-after death.

Examples:

1. Meet Julie, a dear colleague of mine. Julie is a respected physician, a wife and a non-religious person.

A few years ago, Julie had a life-threatening medical condition for which she was admitted to the ICU at the hospital. At one point, her condition became so critical that she became comatose. Slowly, she recovered. Later, she shared this experience with me.

At one point during her coma, she saw herself leaving her body, floating around in space and "it was so peaceful." She also saw one of her patients, floating around and waving at her.

After her recovery, she followed up on this patient. Julie was shocked to discover that this patient had been admitted to the ICU at the time she was in the ICU. This patient died while she was in her coma.

2. Meet Susan again. Later in her life, Susan was under a lot of stress due to her relationship with a man who was an emotional wreck. He did not get along with anyone. Finally, the emotional stress got to a point that Susan decided she would not put up with her boyfriend any more. Soon afterwards, she became mentally confused and was taken to the hospital, where she stayed in a state of amnesia for about nine hours. She was thoroughly evaluated by a neurologist and was given the diagnosis of "Transient Global Amnesia." Her imaging studies of the brain, CT and MRI were unremarkable.

During this state of amnesia, Susan went to a place which she describes as "beautiful and extremely peaceful." She saw other people who were joyful. She was aware of them, but could not communicate with them.

During this period of amnesia, Susan did not remember who the president of the United States was, who her children were and who her boyfriend was. She was in a total disconnect with the human world. Then, she felt this deep emotion of caring for her boyfriend, who would be lost without her, as he did not get along with anyone. This deep emotion brought her back, although she was ready to let go of this world and stay at that "peaceful place." Later, she learned that her boyfriend was praying very deeply for her to come back during her state of amnesia.

My Thoughts About Near-Death Experiences

During normal wakefulness, we stay in the grip of the busy mind most of the time. In other words, our REAL Self (soul) mostly stays in the grip of the thinking mind, which is the activity of the thin, superficial layer of the brain called the cerebral cortex.

During a near-death experience, this mental chatter comes to a stop. Then, the REAL Self (soul) gets in touch with the eternal peace of REAL GOD, residing inside you and all around you. The REAL Self has not completely abandoned the body yet. Therefore, the brain continues to provide images embedded in it of persons or some iconic religious figures or places, etc. That's why religious people see images of their religious figures, which obviously vary from religion to religion. For the same reason, Julie saw the figure of her patient exactly as she remembered him when he was alive.

The REAL Self (soul) gets tarnished with emotions, as we observed earlier. Therefore, it responds to emotional attachments, such as prayers of loved ones, which send out signals in the form of emotional energy. If emotional energy, in the form of prayer as well as emotional attachment to loved ones, is very strong, then the REAL Self may not completely abandon the body, provided the body still has the energy of life.

Section Two

Wake Up While You Can

Chapter **13**

How to Be Stress-free In This life And In Life After Death

As I discussed earlier, what type of new life form a tarnished REAL Self will take, simply follows the rule of Probability. At any given moment, an incredibly huge number of life forms are being born. For example, just consider how many ants, bees and mosquitoes are out there. Therefore, the tarnished REAL Self can be *reborn* as any one of the life forms: a bird, an insect, a fish, a reptile, a human, etc. In this way, you have an incredibly low probability to be reborn as a human.

Can you truly appreciate how lucky you are to be reborn as a human being? You have the greatest opportunity to *wake up* in this lifespan, and get rid of all the emotional burden you have been carrying from lifespan to lifespan and life-after-death to life-after-death.

Why do I say that it is your greatest opportunity to wake up and be free of the piles and piles of emotional burden? That is because human beings have the most evolved brain. Consequently, they have developed what we call logic. In my observation, animals don't have this great asset.

It is this logic that can liberate you from the heavy burden of emotions. Therefore, it is only as a human that you have the chance to cleanse your tarnished REAL Self and end the cycle of rebirths. Then, you are stress-free in this life and in life after death.

Let us use this great tool of logic and find out: What is the root cause of stress in this life and in life after death?

The answer is our emotions. Anger, hate, bitterness, jealousy, guilt and fear are the emotions that cause a huge amount of stress for us during our present lifespan and during our life after death. How about good emotions? Even good emotions such as happiness and love are short lived and easily change into sadness and hate.

Often, emotions lead to emotional actions, which usually cause more stress for everyone involved.

What is the Basis of Emotions?

Use logic, and you will see that an emotion is triggered by a "thought." For example, the emotion of fear is triggered by a "frightening thought." The emotion of fear then influences your thought process, which becomes more frightful. Then, it generates more emotions of fear. Thus, a vicious cycle sets in: thoughts generate fear and fear generates more thoughts.

This vicious cycle can induce certain neurochemical changes in your brain, as well as release the hormones adrenaline and cortisol from the adrenal glands. All of these chemical changes give rise to manifestations of fear, which range from insomnia, anxiety and phobias to panic attacks, allergies and autoimmune disorders.

What Is The Basis Of Thoughts?

It is pretty clear that thoughts give rise to emotions. Where do thoughts come from? While pondering over this question one day, I made a simple, yet profound observation. We humans, always think in terms of a language. For example, if you know English and no other language, you will always think in English, not in Chinese, French or Hindi. Just observe it right now, yourself.

In order to think, you need to know a language. Therefore, language is the basis of thoughts.

What Is The Basis Of Language?

Obviously, the next question is where does the language come from? You are not born with it, right? You learn it as you grow up in a society. You learn it from your parents, teachers, siblings, friends and various tools such as books, electronic devices and sometimes, certain other techniques.

What Is A Language?

Let's use logic and explore what is a language. It is a means to communicate with each other. A language is comprised of words, right? And each word has a concept attached to it. In reality, every word is a sound. For example, listen to a language you don't know. All you will hear is sounds, sounds that make no sense. In order to make sense, you need to know the concepts attached to the sounds. In this way, we can say that a word consists of a sound and an attached concept. Even written language has concepts attached to words. Even Sign language has concepts attached to signs.

What Is The Basis Of Concepts?

Let's use logic and find out where concepts come from. Concepts are the creation of a society, aren't they? When you grow up in a society, your parents teach you the language of that society. They start out by making a sound and point to a person or some object. They keep repeating it until you make a *connection* between that sound and the person or object.

As you grow up in a society, you are *bombarded* with concepts that the society has created, such as the concepts of success, failure, achievement, money, fame, desirable,

59

undesirable, morality, etiquette, responsibility, culture, customs, religion, nationality, past, future, security etc. Based on these concepts, you judge/interpret every person, event and object to be good or bad. Judging triggers the corresponding emotion: good or bad. In this way, concepts create all kind of emotional stress for you.

Who Is Thinking?

If you pay attention, you realize it is always "I" who judges others, who blames others, who is afraid of this and that, etc. It is the "I" who is thinking. Who is this "I"? We need to figure this out, if we truly want to be free of stress.

The Virtual "I"

Who is this "I" that is constantly thinking and creating stress? You may reply, "Oh! It's me." Really?

Let's take a look at this "I". Can you show me where is it? It's in your head, isn't it? It's an abstraction, an illusion, and a phantom. It is a *virtual* entity in your head that *steals* your identity. It is not the "true" you at all. Why do I say that? Because, you are not born with this. In order to know your "True, REAL Self," observe little babies, just a day or so old, as I mentioned earlier in the book.

To recap, little babies are *joyful* from within as soon as their basic physical needs are met (i.e. a full stomach, a clean diaper and a warm blanket). They *smile* and go to sleep. They have no *past* or *future*. They are *not* worried if mom will be around for the next feed. If they did, they wouldn't be able to go to sleep. They don't think. Hence, there are no concepts, no judging, no anger, no *worries*. That's why they have no problem going to sleep. They are so *vulnerable*, but *fear* remains miles away. There is a total *lack of control,* but *no fear* whatsoever.

Once their stomach is full, they *don't* want any more food. If you were to force more food than they need, they would regurgitate. They eat to satisfy their hunger and that's all. *Wanting more* does not exist and that's why they are so *content*. You could feed them breast milk, cow's milk or formula. To them, it doesn't matter as long as it agrees with their stomach and satisfies their hunger.

They don't say, "I don't like your milk, Mom. I like formula better." You would not hear, "Mom, you wrapped me in a pink blanket with butterflies on it. I'm a boy. Therefore, I need a blue blanket with pictures of dinosaurs on it."

They are joyful just looking around. They truly *live in the Now spontaneously* without making an effort to live in the Now. They live in the NOW, because they don't have a busy mind. In fact, newborn babies do not think at all. Why do I say newborn babies don't think? Because, you always think in terms of a language. Newborns know *no* language. Hence, we can conclude newborn babies don't think. They also have no concepts. Why? Because, concepts arise out of language. No language - no concepts.

Newborn babies don't like or dislike someone because of their color, religion, nationality or wealth. That's because they have *not* acquired any *concepts* about race, religion, nationality, history or money. *Concepts* do not exist at all. *Likes and dislikes* do not exist. There are no *preferences or judgments.* No *embarrassment or shame.*

No anger, no hate, no wanting more, no prejudices, no fear...just pure joy, contentment and peace. This is the True Human Nature. I like to call it the "REAL Self," the self that you and I and everyone else on the planet are born with.

Now let's see what happens to this fearless, joyful and peaceful baby.

The Acquired Self

Gradually, another self develops as you grow up in a society. This, we can call the *Acquired Self*. You *acquire* it as a result of *psychosocial conditioning*, from your parents, your school and then, your society in general. This self is conceptual, virtual, and UNREAL.

As a grown-up, all you see is this Acquired Self. You identify with this Acquired Self. *That's who you think you are.* **This becomes the virtual "I" sitting in your head.** Your identity gets *hijacked* by the Acquired Self. Instead of seeing the hijacker for what it is, you think that's who you are. How ironic!

This Acquired Self is the basis for all of your stress. It reacts to outside triggers, which it calls stressors and blames them for your stress. In fact, it is the Acquired Self who reacts to triggers and creates stress for you. In this way, the real source of all stress actually resides insides you. It is good to know this very basic fact. Why? Because if the source of stress is inside you, so is the solution.

This Acquired Self torments you and creates stress even when there is no stressful situation. It conveniently creates *hypothetical* situations (the What If Syndrome) to make you fearful. I like to call it a *monster*, as it is quite frightening and appears strong, but in the end, it is really only virtual.

Sadly, you don't even have a clue what's going on, because you completely identify with the Acquired Self, the *mastermind* behind all of your stress. You could call it the *enemy within*.

In the total grip of the monstrous Acquired Self, you suffer and suffer and create stress not only for yourself, but for others as well.

Chapter 14

The Making Of The Acquired Self/ The Virtual "I"

Where does the Acquired Self come from? It comes from psychosocial conditioning from your society as you grow up. In this way, your Acquired Self is the *offspring* of your society, which itself is a collective Acquired Self we can call the Society's Collective Acquired Self.

Your Acquired Self starts with the virtual "I", which is actually a <u>concept</u> that gets downloaded into your head. Your parents carefully select a <u>label</u> for you. They call it your name, which is basically a sound. Your parents utter this sound as they point towards you. After doing it repeatedly, they finally succeed in drilling into your head that you are indeed Peter, Sarah, Ali or Rekha. At the same time, they also drill in the concepts of Mama and Dada.

As you grow up in a society, you acquire more and more concepts, which circle around the concept of "I," just like the layers of an onion.

How Your Acquired Self Creates Stress For You

Once your Acquired Self *steals* your identity, it *runs* your life. Then, you experience life through the *filters* created by your

Acquired Self. These filters come from concepts, knowledge, information and experiences. The experiences can be your own as well as the experiences of others (virtual experiences for you), in the form of stories and opinions you saw in newspapers, books, magazines, TV or the internet or heard from friends and family.

Basically, your Acquired Self wants to live a very secure life. It wants security. Why? This is because it is *inherently* insecure. It is *not* real. It is virtual, a phantom, an illusion, but it thinks it is real and it wants to live forever. Pretty crazy, isn't it?

In order to be safe, your Acquired Self *interprets* every experience (real experience or virtual experience. It doesn't matter) based on the information stored in it and *judges* the experience to be good or bad, which triggers an emotion, whether good or bad. Then, it *stores* the entire experience along with the triggered emotion into your *memory* box, where it stays *alive*, even years later. This is how your Acquired Self creates your *memories* or the <u>past</u>. Based on the past, it creates some more thoughts it calls "My Future."

Stress Created by the "Past and Future"

By keeping the old *dead* events alive, your Acquired Self keeps the *fire* of old emotions burning inside you. It calls them "my past" and "my memories". It judges these memories as either good or bad.

By replaying bad memories, your Acquired Self continues to experience the *negative* emotions attached to these memories in the form of *humiliation, anger, hate, bitterness, jealousy and revenge.*

By replaying good memories, your Acquired Self starts to *miss* those wonderful experiences and becomes *sad*.

The Acquired Self Wants to Change Its Past

Here's another interesting phenomenon. The Acquired Self wants to control the virtual world of memories. It is strongly attached to sweet memories, but it wants to run away from bad memories Therefore, it tries to modify the stories and events.

For example:

"If my teacher hadn't humiliated me in front of entire class, I'd be a happy person today."

"Why didn't I see the clues? He's been cheating on me all along! Why did I marry him?"

"Why did I take this job? My boss is so stingy and demanding."

"Why didn't I sell my stocks six months ago when the financial market was so high?"

But of course, the Acquired Self can't change what has already happened. It feels *annoyed, frustrated, angry* and sometimes *guilty* as well. The more it tries to change those painful memories, the stronger they get. What an irony!

The Acquired Self wants to Secure a Happy Future

In addition, the Acquired Self doesn't want any bad event to happen again, ever! It wants perfect *security*. Your Acquired Self has been conditioned to learn from the past. Therefore, it wants to create a perfect world for itself in which there are only good things, and bad things do not exist. It wants to create a paradise for itself. Therefore, it continues to generate new thoughts along the lines of how to prevent bad events from happening again.

The "What If" Syndrome

But then another thought erupts: *"What if I can't prevent it from happening again?"* That triggers huge *fear and anxiety.*

Caught up in the "What if, What may, What will I do Syndrome," your Acquired Self creates a virtual movie. In this way, it creates a huge amount of *fear* in you. In the pursuit of security and peace, your Acquired Self *robs* you of any peace of mind you had. How counterproductive!

Some examples:

"What if I lose my job again?"

"What if my boss insults me again?"

"What if I become fat again?"

"What if I lose it again?"

"What if I get stung by the bee again?"

"What if my audience makes fun of me again?"

"What if I become poor again?"

"What if I lose my friends again?"

"What if I get dumped again?"

"What if I'm late again?"

"What if I miss my flight again?"

"What if no one pays attention to me again?"

"What if my husband cheats again?"

"What if I have an attack of asthma again?"

In reality, those situations don't exist at all. In other words, your Acquired Self is so *insecure* and *afraid* of its own death, that it creates all *possible,* dreadful case scenarios and tries to *figure out* how it can *escape* its death in every possible way. In doing so, it creates tons of *unnecessary* fear for you.

The Acquired Self Creates Attachment And Avoidance

Experiences that are labeled good, your Acquired Self wants *more* of and the ones labeled bad, it wants to *run* away from. This is the basis of psychological *attachment* and *avoidance.* Attachment is also called *positive* attachment and avoidance is also called *negative* attachment

Your Acquired Self gets very *attached* to good experiences, such as praise and validation, which provides a *temporary* relief from its insecurity. That's why your Acquired Self gets attached to the concepts of *money*, *power, success and beauty*, all of which bring it praise and validation and provides *temporary rel*ief from insecurity.

Your Acquired Self also gets *praise* from family, friends and fans regarding its success, fame and accomplishments. It wants more and more of these experiences. It also feels *validated* when it is related, bonded or responsible for someone. For example, if you own a pet, it *validates* the existence of you as an owner and provides your Acquired Self temporary relief from insecurity. That's why it doesn't want to ever *lose* its pets, family, friends and fans. *Even the idea of losing them rips through the paper-thin layer of security and stirs up deep-seated, inherent insecurity, which triggers a huge amount of fear.*

Your Acquired Self also seeks validation through conceptual identities such as a doctor, lawyer, teacher, political, social or religious leader, movie star, employee of a certain company, citizen of a certain country, member of a certain

67

social, political or religious group, etc. That's why even the thought of losing its virtual identity creates a huge amount of fear. This is why you are so afraid of the possibility of losing your professional license, career, citizenship, elections, etc.

Your Acquired Self does not *ever* want to *lose* anything or anyone that is "Mine." That would mean losing a part of "Mine." How terrible that would be! That's why it is afraid of losing possessions. The more possessions you have as "My, Mine," the more you *fear* losing them and the more you try to protect them. You may end up living in a gated community to protect your belongings. Even news of someone getting robbed creates a lot of fear for you.

In addition, your Acquired Self wants to *avoid* unpleasant experiences, such as failure, punishment, loneliness, humiliation, poverty, aging, disease and death at all costs. *Even the thought of such unpleasant experiences triggers intense fear.*

Acquired Self Interprets Every Situation/Person

Your Acquired Self also quickly wants to *interpret* every situation it encounters and every person it meets, based upon its *stored* information. Why? Because, it wants to feel secure. It quickly judges if a person is safe or unsafe, based upon their appearance, without even exchanging a word. Judging triggers emotion. For example if it judges a person to be unsafe, you will start to experience fear, even though the other person has not done anything to you.

Often, it doesn't want to take any chances, so it won't interact with anyone it doesn't know. You may remember, "don't talk to strangers" from your childhood. You also want to make sure to download this very important message into the growing Acquired Self of your children. Maybe you read a story about some girl who got abducted by a stranger in a far place you know nothing about. It rips through your feeling of security. Ironically, it reinforces your self-fulfilling prophecy of being "fearful of strangers." Obviously, you don't hear or pay attention to the countless safe encounters with strangers.

The Acquired Self Creates Expectations

Your Acquired Self is downloaded with the concept of, "how others should and shouldn't behave towards you and how you should and shouldn't behave towards them." For example, you expect certain kinds of behavior from your spouse, parents, brothers, sisters, friends and colleagues and *vice versa*. In a way, society dictates how each of us should fulfill our role. We can call it the *book of role descriptions,* written by the Collective Acquired Self of Society. Each and every person living in a particular society is downloaded with this *book of role descriptions*.

Everyone knows the description of his/her role and also knows the description of the role of others. For example, this book tells you *how a wife should behave, how a husband should behave, how a parent should behave, how a friend should behave, how a child should behave, how a teacher should behave, how a doctor should behave, etc.* Automatically it gives rise to certain expectations.

You *expect* others to play their part right, by the book. They *expect* you to play your role right. Now what happens if someone doesn't play his part right? You get frustrated and at times, angry. It's actually your Acquired Self who feels let down, frustrated and angry, because it is the Acquired Self who builds up expectations. Your Acquired Self believes in all of the concepts contained in the book of role descriptions.

The closer the relationship, the higher the expectations... And more emotional pain if someone does not meet your expectations. This emotional pain manifests as annoyances, frustrations and anger.

Examples:

- *A spouse falling off the ladder of expectations is the most frequent cause of divorce. It goes something like this: In a marriage, as soon as the period of intense sexual romance has cooled, the deeper layers of two Acquired Selves show their faces. Now each spouse starts seeing faults in the other person, as the person is not living up to expectations. This initially causes annoyance, which continues to build up in the memory box and eventually leads to pain and anger. Then one day, there is a big blow up and the marriage ends up in a divorce.*

- *Brothers, sisters and close friends get mad and angry if their expectations are not met. Sometimes they end up losing lifelong relationships.*

- *Kids failing to meet the expectations of their parents cause a lot of pain and suffering for their parents as well as themselves. For example, parents expected their son to become a doctor, but the son got poor grades in school. This caused severe headaches and ugly arguments between the son and his parents.*

- *Parents expected their daughter to marry someone they thought suitable for her, but she married someone else. Another cause for anger and pain.*

- *A wife expected a gift on her birthday but didn't get anything. The result? Hurt, pain and anger.*

- *A husband expected his wife to be nice to his rowdy buddies, but she called them immature dirt bags, which caused a huge argument, pain and anger.*

- *An employee expected a raise but didn't get one, which caused pain and resentment.*

- *A person expected wonderful golden years after*

retirement, but ended up having cancer, which resulted in bitterness and anger, in addition to the pain of the news of cancer.

- *In addition to their own personal life, people also build expectations around political and religious figures, movie stars, singers, artists, etc. and get very disappointed and angry if their icon doesn't live up to their expectations. Some even get so angry that they end up killing their icon.*

- *People also create expectations around political, economic and religious systems and get very upset once their expectations are not fulfilled.*

- *People even have expectations about, "how long they will live." It is called **life expectancy**. We feel cheated if someone close to us dies before they were supposed to.*

The Collective Acquired Self of Society promises you that you will be rewarded if you follow the rules and punished if you don't. Now what happens if you follow the rules and don't get rewarded and someone who doesn't follow the rules gets rewarded? You get very upset and angry.

For example, you are an honest person suffering economic hardships while some crooked, dishonest liar is rolling in money. "Life isn't fair" you may find yourself saying. You feel very disappointed and angry at life.

The Acquired Self Creates Self-righteousness

Another common reason for anger and frustration is self-righteousness.

What is self-righteousness? In simple terms it means, "I am right." It also *implies* that "you are wrong." This is the root cause of all disagreements, disputes, arguments, quarrels, fights, lawsuits, battles and wars, all of which obviously create a huge amount of anger.

With few exceptions, everyone suffers from self-righteousness. Interestingly, people don't like to be called self-righteous because it's considered a bad quality. They don't think they are self-righteous, but they readily see it in others. They simply judge others to be self-righteous and don't go any deeper. Actually, they believe they are *right* that someone else is self-righteous. Interesting, isn't it?

Self-righteousness is an extremely common affliction and one of the reasons for all human conflicts. If we want to understand human conflicts, it makes sense to look at self-righteousness more deeply.

What is the Basis of Self-Righteousness?

Why do we believe that we are right and others are wrong? For example, for the same event, different people will have different opinions. Each one believes that he is right and others are wrong. The event is the same, but its interpretations are very different. Obviously, the problem lies in the interpretations. Now who is it that is doing the interpretation? It's your Acquired Self, isn't it?

Typically when a person looks at an event, his Acquired Self *interprets* that event against the background of the already stored information in his conditioned mind. Obviously, this stored information varies from person to person. Therefore, interpretation of the same event varies from person to person. Most people are in the grip of their Acquired Selves. Therefore, they strongly believe that their interpretation of the event is *right*.

If we look deeper at the composition of a person's Acquired Self, we find that the *book of role descriptions* is an important part of it. This book, as we observed earlier, describes how a person *should* and *should not* behave in a given society. In addition to creating expectations, it also provides a background against which everyone keeps *judging* others' behavior. It tells you and everyone else "what is *right* and what is *wrong*"; "what is *virtue* and what is *evil*." This is the basis of *morality*.

In addition to the *book of role descriptions*, your Society also downloads into your Acquired Self, many other concepts. For example, it gives you the concepts about "your rights," "human rights," "animal rights," "traffic rules," "sports rules," All of these concepts become part of your Acquired Self and give you more ammunition to be *right*. These concepts strengthen your self-righteousness.

When you are in the grip of your Acquired Self, theses concepts and rules become your *beliefs*. When others don't follow the rules, you get frustrated and angry. For example, you are on the road, following the traffic rules and some other driver does not. Your Acquired Self judges you to be right and the other person to be wrong. This makes you furious. This is the basis of road rage, which can, sometimes, lead to physical violence.

In addition, your Society downloads into your Acquired Self the knowledge of history, which primarily is an interpretation of certain events by the Acquired Self of the historian-writer. That is the reason why there are so many different interpretations of the same events and of course, every historian believes he is right. The historian's interpretation of events becomes part of your Acquired Self and you believe them to be absolutely true (although the event may have happened before you and the historian were even born). Different Acquired Selves with different versions of the same historic event or historic figure then get into heated arguments and get angry at each other.

With this background, your Acquired Self also judges current political, social, cultural events. Usually, it is some so called expert who does it for you, on a TV show, in a newspaper or in a book. Acquired Selves with different versions of history interpret current events differently and each one believes he is right. With this background, people get into heated arguments and get mad and angry at each other.

It is interesting to note that in a given society, there are collective concepts about what is right and what is wrong. This creates a *collective self-righteousness*, which gets reinforced constantly by the news media in that society. *What is right in one society may be wrong in another society.* This creates conflict between various societies. That's why people living in one society get angry at another society. This is the basis of *collective conflict, anger and violence* between various nations.

Then, within a given society, there are various concepts about what is right and what is wrong, depending upon various social, political and religious groups in that society. This creates conflict, anger and violence between various groups within a society.

Then within a group, there are various concepts about what is right and what is wrong. Therefore, within the same group, people get angry and fight among each other. Even within a family, there are various concepts about what is right and what is wrong. It leads to conflict, anger and violence (usually verbal but sometimes even physical) between various members of the same family. For example, your husband may believe in disciplining the kids and you don't. This could lead to a serious argument and verbal conflict.

Then, within an individual, there are conflicting concepts what is right and what is wrong. There is one code of ethics for the work place and another one for home, one code of ethics for friends and another one for enemies, one standard for yourself and another one for everyone else.

It all boils down to "I". Based on the concepts attached to virtual "I", your Acquired Self, you judge everyone else out there as either your friend or enemy. That's how you perceive other people - as either your friends or your enemies: at home, in your neighborhood, at your work place, in your social, political or religious group, in your country and in the world. You stay annoyed and angry with your enemies, which often leads to violence, verbal as well as physical.

The Acquired Self Reacts To Insults

Another reason why people get angry is *insults.* Obviously, you get angry when someone insults you. You *may or may not* express your anger.

Many people fight back by returning insulting remarks or gestures. Also, there are those who *pretend* to be polite and civilized on the surface, while fuming with anger underneath. Later, they often express their anger while talking to their spouse or friends. Some even suppress anger so deeply that on the surface, they *manage* to remain polite and civilized all the time. They may even try to *fake* a smile, but deep inside, they feel irritated and don't even know why they feel that way!

What is the Basis of Insults?

Is it possible for you to *never* be insulted? I'm not talking about suppressing your anger and pretending that you are not insulted, but in reality - to not actually feel insulted at all when someone insults you.

In order to be truly free of insults, you first need to figure out, "who is it inside you who gets insulted in the first place."

Use logic and you will find that it's your Acquired Self who gets insulted. *The True Self never gets insulted*. Why do I say that? This is because a newborn baby never gets insulted. *You can try to insult a baby by saying whatever you want, but the baby will not be insulted*. In the same way, imagine someone trying to insult you in a language or through gestures that you don't understand. Obviously, you will *not* be insulted. Therefore, we can conclude that for the insult to occur, one has to understand the *concepts* attached to those words and gestures. Otherwise, they have no power.

Where do you learn the words and gestures and all of the concepts attached to them? You are not born with them. You obviously learn them as you grow up in a certain society. That's why it is logical to conclude it's your Acquired Self who gets insulted.

With every word, there is a concept attached. For example, the word STUPID has a whole concept of unintelligence, inadequacy and worthlessness attached to it. When your developing Acquired Self learns this word, it stores all the negative concepts attached to the word. When someone calls you by that word, the negative concept attached to that word is activated and negative thoughts trigger negative emotions. You feel unintelligent, worthless, inadequate, which triggers anger. *You didn't deserve it. How dare someone say that to you*? Actually, your Acquired Self's sense of self-esteem is threatened. Therefore, your Acquired Self fights back verbally or even physically in order to secure its existence, its self-esteem.

The insulting words are created by the Society Collective Acquired Self for the individual Acquired Selves to fight with each other, aren't they?

Society's Collective Acquired Self downloads the concept of *"insult and respect"* into your Acquired Self. When others respect you, your Acquired Self feels validated and when others insult you, your Acquired Self feels humiliated. In other words, your Acquired Self is constantly *reacting* to how others treat it.

Your Acquired Self wants to be respected and not be insulted. Obviously, it has no control over others' behavior, but it doesn't know this basic fact. It just keep searching for respect and running away from insult. It is especially true if at an early age you were insulted (teased) a lot. Your Acquired Self felt humiliated and all of those painful experiences become part of your Acquired Self. Then, your Acquired Self found a way (academics, sports, arts, etc.) for others to start respecting you. Your Acquired Self finally got the praise and validation it was so hungry for. Naturally, your Acquired Self works hard on this track and usually ends up being quite accomplished and successful in that field. With each step of success, it gets more respect, praise and validation and it loves it all. *The more it gets attached to respect, the more it resents the idea of insult.* Then, a trivial teasing remark can upset your Acquired Self for days. You may even burst into anger in a social situation where you didn't get enough respect, which you perceive as an insult.

Your Acquired Self Gets In Competition And Comparison

During psychosocial conditioning, *competition and comparison* are drilled into the developing Acquired Self. You see it everywhere, at home, at work, at school, at parties, on TV and practically in every walk of life.

How Competition Creates Stress For You

When you're in competition, you either win or lose. What happens when you win? You get praise, validation and recognition. For that moment, you're the king of the hill. You have this wonderful feeling – a natural high filled with thrill and excitement. A few moments later, it's gone. You want more of it, but the moment, the occasion has passed. Now you have to work hard to be the "king of the hill" again. It takes a lot of hard work to be the champion, the winner, and the outstanding person again.

The more victories you have, the more *addicted* you become to the momentary thrill and excitement. There is no ending. You simply want more and more and keep working in that pursuit. This is how you become greedy.

A competitive mind never gets enough and therefore, is always dissatisfied. You may be a wealthy, powerful, accomplished person, but inside you are empty, unhappy and dissatisfied.

Dissatisfaction leads to more greed for momentary pleasures and that means you must earn more money, fame, recognition, etc. It's a *vicious* cycle, which often leads to various addictions, such as addiction to work, power, career, etc. You have *no* time for your family. Consequences: unhappy spouse, unhappy kids and often *divorce* which causes more emotional pain.

How Comparison Creates Stress For You

Comparison lies at the root of ego. *"I am better than the others because of so and so."* The Society's Collective Acquired Self provides you with plenty of reasons to feel better than others. These ego-maker concepts include wealth, success, fame, knowledge, culture, genealogy, heritage, possessions, looks, appearances, religious, political and social clubs, etc.

Locked in the prison of ego, you feel quite miserable. On the surface, you're accomplished, famous and successful, but deep inside you feel empty, jealous and irritated. When society makes you feel *special* by acknowledging your success, your heroic actions or your special talents, you get a momentary thrill and excitement, but then it *fades* away... And you want more. You are never satisfied. You can't get enough praise, validation or recognition. You always want more.

Society of course, can't provide you with praise and recognition all the time. Often, it starts criticizing you as well. *First it builds you up and then it brings you down.* Then you feel miserable. You want others, especially your close friends and family members, to like you for your accomplishments and achievements. Instead, they generally stop liking you because they don't approve of the way you act under the influence of your ego.

An egocentric person is in the total grip of his own Acquired Self. He interacts with the world from the *virtual* castle of his own grandiosity. Why and how is this castle of grandiosity built? The Acquired Self builds this virtual castle in the pursuit of emotional security. It wants to suppress the fire of insecurity and worthlessness. It wants to be someone that everyone praises, validates and acknowledges instead of mocking, humiliating or criticizing.

For example, as a child or as a teenager you were subjected to comparison or criticism by some authority figure, such as your mother or your teacher. You felt the pain of humiliation and worthlessness. You also probably felt that you didn't deserve it. They were simply being *mean* to you. These thoughts of meanness and unfairness provoked intense anger inside you. All of these thoughts and emotions were stored in your memory as a constant nagging voice of criticism.

You may or may not be aware of these humiliating experiences any more. Some of these experiences, especially from early childhood, may have been forgotten. However, in your subconscious mind, these experiences are very much alive.

From these humiliating experiences comes another inner thought, "I'll never be humiliated again" or "I'll prove them wrong!" This inner thought becomes your *drive* to succeed in the world. It makes you work hard. You accomplish a lot, become successful and earn a lot of money and respect.

You get strongly attached to "success," as it validates you and provide a momentary band-aid on the old, but very much alive, wound of humiliation and anger. Attached to your success, you develop a *big* ego. On the surface you are accomplished and successful, but inside you still feel worthless, humiliated, irritated, angry and dissatisfied.

Then, a little thing triggers your inner anger to the surface. You are easily annoyed and have outbursts of anger over things that wouldn't bother other people - things such as someone *not* agreeing with you or making an innocent, unflattering remark. Why does this trigger your anger? Because, you expect them to acknowledge and validate your success. When they don't, you feel like they are *criticizing* you and you over-react with all your piled up anger. This behavior causes you to lose some true friends. You want validation from your friends, but your actions push away your true friends. How ironic!

You keep proving to others and yourself over and over again how great you are, but it's never enough to heal your inner wound of worthlessness, unfairness and anger.

Actually, the more successful you become, the bigger your *ego* becomes and the more easily you get angry over little things.

Some people may not have gone through (or may not remember) humiliating experiences. However, they (their Acquired Self) learn from the Society's Collective Acquired Self that success, money, power or connections with powerful people are very important to live a "successful life" and they start to believe in this delusion. You (your Acquired Self) get praise and validation through your success, accomplishments, money, power, possessions, looks, etc. Each time it gets validated, its inner insecurity temporarily subsides, so it feels thrilled and excited. Unfortunately, all of this vanishes quickly and then it wants more... And the circus goes on!

Ego can take another form that most people are unaware of. Many people get attached to failures, losses and misery, either due to their own experiences (losses in competition and comparison) or collective losses of their collective identity (such as a religious, cultural or political groups). Then they (their Acquired Self) feel *special* in being a failure or miserable... the famous "Martyr Syndrome."

The Acquired Self Leaves You With *No* Time

People often complain they have *no* time. They are so busy with their life that they have *no* time to relax, *no* time to go for a walk, *no* time to prepare their meals, etc.

Have you ever looked at where your time goes? Look at your activities during the daytime *objectively* and you will find out where do you end up spending your time.

In the grip of your Acquired Self, most people want to make more and more money. In the pursuit of "making more money" you end up working day and night, which is often full of demands and challenges. A lot of individuals also *commit* to a number of social obligations, which are also demanding and time-consuming. But in the end there is a reward, recognition, praise, which your Acquired Self is so hungry for. Therefore, you continue to work day and night and carry on your social obligations as well.

Then you suffer from the "No Time Syndrome." You find yourself on the run. You stay rushed, agitated and restless. You don't have any time to prepare your meals. You grab a quick breakfast, often cereal, as you don't have any time to cook your meal. You may even drive through a restaurant to grab your meal and eat it inside your car while driving. Often, you have to travel a lot. Then you grab your meals at the airports, whatever you can find, which is often unhealthy fast food.

Another reason why people don't have any time is their *addiction* to "entertainment" in one form or another. Even after a long day, people come home, and turn their TV on or go straight to their computers to get entertainment. It is actually a great escape, your Society's Collective Acquired Self teaches you in order to *decompress* from the stress of daily living, which is in fact, created by the Society's Collective Acquired Self. Interesting, isn't it!

At some point during entertainment activities, you may suddenly realize it's time for dinner. Then you think of something you can prepare fast: a frozen dinner, a pizza, hot dogs etc, that you can throw in the microwave, while you go back to your *screen* of entertainment.

Chitchatting is another common black hole of time. Watch yourself how much time you spend chitchatting face-to-face, on the phone, on the Internet, etc.

As a result of "rat-race for money," social obligations, entertainment activities and chitchatting, you are left with *no time* to prepare your meals, eat your food in peace or go for a walk. You are always in a rush. This is one of the main reasons why your blood sugars stay high.

The Acquired Self Keeps You Trapped In Partying

Most people get off their diet and indulge in unhealthy eating behavior during parties. Under the social pressure, you *cave in* and end up eating large amount of food, which is often unhealthy stuff.

Why do you end up *sabotaging* your good eating habits? Pay attention and you will see you lose all control on your eating when you are in a party. It is as if, some inner *monster* takes you over and lures you into all sorts of unhealthy foods. This is your Acquired self, isn't it.

Starting from a young age, your Society's Collective Acquired Self downloads into your personal Acquired Self, a long list of *special* days that *must* be celebrated with food, often very unhealthy food: birthdays, religious and national holidays and anniversaries are some examples. In addition, there are many other opportunities for celebrations. In general, the more successful you are, the more parties you go to and the more you end eating unhealthy food.

All parties are *centered* a round unhealthy foods and often a lot of food. Parties are also a lot of fun. In this way, Society's Collective Acquired Self downloads the concept of "food and fun" into your growing Acquired Self, since early childhood. You stay in this *mental* prison for the rest of your life.

After partying, you see your blood sugars as well as your weight going up. You don't like it. You feel like a big failure. You also feel *guilty* of cheating. You promise one more time to yourself to stay *disciplined* with your diet, which you are able to do until the next round of parties and you fall off the wagon, again.

The Acquired Self Creates All Of Your Stress

It is pretty clear that your Acquired Self creates all of your stress. The Virtual "I" sitting at the core of your Acquired Self, looks at life through the *filters* of concepts, ideas, rules, information, past and future, which triggers a burden of emotional stress. Emotions then taint your thoughts. Emotional thoughts trigger more emotional distress.

A *vicious* cycle of, thought-emotion-thought sets in. This is the basis of worrying, anxiety, anger, frustrations, hate, revenge, jealousy, guilt, thrill and excitement, greed, agitation, restlessness, sadness, and depression.
Then, actions arise out of emotional thoughts, which often cause more stress for yourself and the others. The actions may be verbal, written or physical.

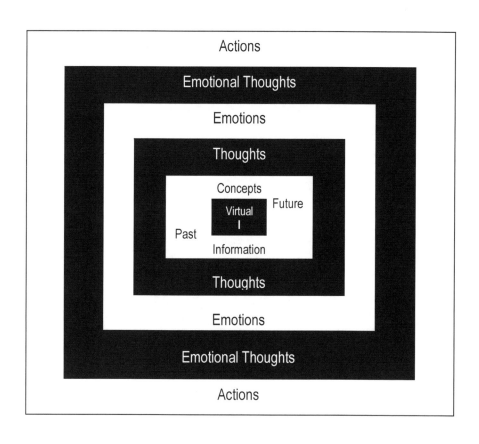

The Acquired Self

Chapter 15

How To Be Free Of Your Acquired Self

Acquired Self is obviously the root cause of all of your emotional stress. The obvious question is: how to be free of your Acquired Self?

A word of caution: Don't try to *control* or *discipline* your Acquired Self. This strategy simply *strengthens* your Acquired Self and creates more stress. Also do not start to dislike/hate your Acquired Self. This creates a *negative* attachment, which would further strengthen the grip of your Acquired Self on you.

See Acquired Self for what it is. In fact, Acquired Self is a *tool* to function in the society. It's only when it steals your identity-you mistakenly think that's who you are, that it gets in the driver's seat, takes control of your thoughts, emotions and actions and creates all of the emotional stress for you.

Therefore, you need to rise above your Acquired Self. Then, you can utilize it as a tool to function in society and put it to rest when it is not needed.

First of all, you have to see your Acquired Self as *separate* from you. Only then, can you see it for what it is. However, if you continue to *identify* with your Acquired Self, you can *never* see its true colors. As long as you and your Acquired Self are *stuck* together, obviously you can *never* be free of it.

In order to *free* yourself from your Acquired Self, you have to see it in action. When you're in the grip of your Acquired Self, you *immediately* react to *triggers*. We can call it <u>autopilot</u> mode. These automatic reactions often cause more stress for you and others. Later on, when you come to your senses, you often *regret* what you said or did.

1. Pause!

The *first step* to *separate* yourself from your Acquired Self is to *not* let it automatically control your actions. Pause! Stop for a moment, before you *react* to what you heard, read or watched.

2. Shift Your Awareness/Attention To The Now

Shift your attention to the *Now*. What is Now? Now is *not* what is in your head, but what is in front of your eyes. It is your <u>field of awareness</u>.

Pause for a moment right now and pay attention to what you see, what you hear, what you smell, what you taste and what you touch. Don't think, just sense.

In general, when we see, we only pay attention to objects without paying any attention to the *space* in which everything is. Without space, there would be no objects. So when you see objects, also be aware of the space which gives rise to all objects. Also when you see some movement, be aware of *stillness* in the background. In the same way, when you listen, also pay attention to the *silence*, without which there would be no sound.

Use your eyes and ears and be aware of *space, stillness, silence*, which gives rise to all objects, events and sounds.

Practice to be aware of the Now. Then, you can easily *shift* your attention to the *Now* as soon as you realize your thoughts and emotions have taken you over.

The moment you switch your attention to the Now, you are free of your thoughts and their associated emotions. In other words, you are free of your Acquired Self. *Instantaneously,* you will feel *relief* from anger, fear or any other stressful emotion. That's how powerful this seemingly simple step is. A moment later, your attention may again be *sucked* up by the thoughts and emotions. It's okay. Simply keep shifting your attention/awareness into the Now.

Your Acquired Self needs your *attention* to thrive. That's why it *sucks* up your attention/awareness most of the time. However, you have the power to *switch* gears and *divert* your attention/awareness to the Now. Without your attention/awareness, your Acquired Self can *no* longer survive. As long as your attention/awareness is in the Now, you are *free* of the Acquired Self.

Remember this phrase: <u>Keep your mind where your body is</u>.

While fully aware of the Now, feel and watch the drama your Acquired Self creates. Don't run away from it. After a little while, it will settle down.

<u>Example:</u>

You're stuck in traffic on your way to the airport. You start worrying. "What if I miss my flight? Then you may point finger at your spouse, "Only if you had listened to me to leave on time, we wouldn't be in this mess. You *never* listen to me anyway." Your spouse *fires* back with some *ugly* words that trigger more anger inside you. Engaged in the verbal fight, you both get upset and angry. Then you may see some driver *not* following the traffic rules. You may *yell* at him and get into a road rage. You may get so angry from the drama that your Acquired Self creates, that you may end up having chest pain and find yourself heading to a hospital...Or you can choose to shift your attention from thoughts to the Now: Watch the car in front of you, the cars to each side, the median of the freeway, the electric poles seemingly running backwards, the sky, the clouds, etc. Also pay attention to your breathing, which is a *continuous* act in the Now. Chances are pretty good that you will arrive at the airport safely, certainly without any anger or high blood pressure or high blood sugar. You may or may not be late. If you are late, you will deal with it. Therefore, live in the Now, stay in reality and you won't have any emotional distress.

Caution:

Be careful *not* to confuse *attention* with *concentration*. Attention is simple awareness, that's all! It is there automatically, without any effort. On the other hand, concentration and discipline require a lot of effort and are quite stressful by themselves.

3. Use Logic

Now take the next step: use *logic*, the most wonderful tool we humans have. Why? Because, the Acquired Self is always *illogical* and can't stand the blazing *torch* of logic. Therefore, use logic and see the *true colors* of your Acquired Self. See for yourself who is really at the root of all of stress. See how *illogical* your Acquired Self is.

For example, you *fume* over things that happened in the past: Someone *insulted* you, *betrayed* you, *let you down,* etc. Use logic and see for yourself that no matter how much you think about your past, you can *never* change it. "But I must learn from it so it must *never* happen to me again," says an inner voice. With that kind of mindset, what people often end up learning is *mistrust, jealousy, hate and revenge*. They also become *fearful* that it may happen again. In fact, you keep your past *alive* (although it has otherwise *died*) as long as you stay in the mindset to *learn* from it. Only when you completely *let go* of your past, you can be *free* of the emotional trauma it caused you.

Emotional pain from the past also comes in another form: *sweet memories*. Even thinking about all the good times makes you *sad*. In fact, the more you think about "sweet memories," the *sadder* you get. Use logic and realize those "sweet memories" are nothing more than an *illusion*, a *dream*, a *phantom*. Those events were "Real" when they happened, but now they are simply a package of *mental pictures*, *stories* and associated *emotions*. Only when you completely *let go* of your "sweet memories," can you be *free* of sadness, caused by them.

Another example: Your Acquired Self may be worried about its future. Use common sense and you'll see whatever your thoughts imply, may or may not happen... But certainly, it's not happening in the Now, in front of your eyes, right? Therefore, it's a phantom, an illusion. How can you really take care of a problem that doesn't even exist? If and when it happens, at "that time, the present moment," you'll be able to take *real* action, instead of the *virtual* action your Acquired Self keeps thinking about, which serves no purpose, but simply generates fear.

Another example: You are in your sixties and doing fine. Then one day, you read in the newspaper that someone important died of cancer. Your Acquired Self triggers a thought. What if I have cancer? This creates another thought of possibly losing your health, autonomy and ultimately dying. This creates a huge amount of fear. You start to feel your heart pounding. You feel uneasiness and anxiety. Then, you start wondering who'll take care of your wife if you die, which further worsens your fear and suddenly, you've got a full-fledged panic attack.

Even in the *midst* of this panic attack, pause, take some deep breaths and start counting your breaths. Look around and see what is actually happening in front of you. Be aware of the space, silence and stillness. Fully realize that it is your Acquired Self that is creating fear. Then, use logic. Ask yourself: Do I have cancer at this moment? Am I losing my autonomy at this moment? You realize you really don't have any problems at this moment. Then, you also clearly see that it is actually your Acquired Self playing tricks with you by creating an imaginary future. The moment you clearly see the Acquired Self for what it is, an entity separate from you, it starts to lose its power over you. Using logic, you also tell your mind: "I will deal with any medical condition, if and when it arises." Make a mental note to discuss it with your doctor on your next visit or even write it down on a piece of paper. You will see fear completely evaporate and you can move on with your everyday life.

In addition, *acknowledge* the basic law of nature: if you are born, then one day you die. There are *no* exceptions to this rule. The Acquired Self however, does not want to die and wishes to live forever. Therefore, it makes death something you must avoid, cheat, conquer, etc. In this way, it creates a lot of *negativity* about death. In the grip of their Acquired Self, many people *worry* about death all their life and then one day they die.

After death, their REAL Self, who has been tarnished with the emotions generated by the Acquired Self, continues to suffer from emotions.

Stop worrying and start living. You can do it once you are free of your Acquired Self.

Instead of worrying, take action in the present moment. For example, eat right, exercise regularly and take vitamin D every day. There's a good chance you won't develop cancer, heart disease or Alzheimer's dementia etc. Even if you do develop any medical condition, you will be able to deal with it at that time.

However, if you just keep worrying and don't take any actions, chances are you may develop these diseases. Take real action in the present moment, instead of worrying about the results.

Next time you find yourself saying," I don't know where all of my time goes. I feel so *pushed* all the time." Use logic and look at all of your activities, engagements and commitments, from a *neutral* ground. Then, figure out what are important

90

activities for basic living and what are the activities for ego-enhancement, thrill, excitement and entertainment.

Next time you are at a party, realize your body has not changed because you are in a party. Eat to satisfy your hunger, not to *appease* your friends and family members.

Use logic and realize special days are special, because the Society's Collective Acquired Self says so. In Real, they are just another day in Nature.

Caution:

Please be aware that I am using the word logic as the simple <u>common sense</u> that every human is born with. I am not using it as intellectualization, rationalization or reasoning.

4. Be Aware Of The Conceptual World We Live In

Have you ever pondered about the world we live in? If you take a fresh, logical look at the human world without preconceived notions, you will find that we live in a *conceptual world*, a *virtual world*, not a real world.

Because everyone around us lives in this collective conceptual, virtual world, we think it is real. Actually, we simply accept it as real and don't even bother investigating whether it is real or not.

For example, let's say you watch the Oscar Awards on TV. Through the goggles of the conditioned mind, (your Acquired Self), you see five actresses nominated for best actress. After a few moments of agony, everyone is told who wins *best actress of the year*. The winner is obviously thrilled and excited, but the other four feel defeated, though they try to force a fake smile. For the winner, the moment has finally arrived, the moment for which she has waited for years. She gets overwhelmed with emotions, but manages to deliver a tearful speech. Then, her moment is over. In a few minutes, it is someone else going through similar emotions.

If you are a serious moviegoer, you have your own opinion as to *"who deserves to be the best actress."* If your choice wins, you are also *thrilled*, but if your choice loses, you will be *disappointed,* sometimes even *angry* and *bitter* about the *unfairness*.

You and the world call it *entertainment*. You want more of it and the world is well equipped to provide you with more! Over the next several days, you enjoy seeing more and more about the whole event on the Internet, TV, newspapers and magazines. You see stories about before and after parties, designer dresses, behind the scenes, etc.

For the next few days, you even talk to your friends about the whole experience and have more fun. Actually, the more you know, the more you can impress your friends and the more special you feel about yourself.

Now, let's look at the whole event from an <u>unconditioned mind - someone without the Acquired Self, or Your REAL Self that is *not* in the grip of the Acquired Self</u>. Now, what you see is a person coming on stage to receive a shiny peace of metal. Holding that piece of metal in her hands, she gets very emotional, her eyes become tearful and her voice chokes. She says a few words and then everyone starts clapping. Why, you wonder?

On the other hand, in the conceptual world, that piece of metal has a huge *concept* attached to it. The woman appearing on stage is not just a woman, but has a huge *concept* attached to her. The whole drama has a huge *concept* attached to it. *The entire concept reverberates with the concept in your head and in everyone else's head, about Oscars, actresses and actors, movies and the concepts of success, achievement, fame, wealth and glamour.*

In other words, your Acquired Self (the *Baby* Monster) gets fed by the *Papa* Monster of society! That's why you enjoy it so much. For you and everyone else, it becomes real. Actually, you don't even question whether it is real or not. You watch and talk about it as if it was real.

It is interesting to know that you may be able to see the superficial, virtual nature of the part of the conceptual world that you are not attached to. For example, if you are attached to sports and not to movies, you may *not* be interested in watching the Oscars and may even realize their superficial nature, but you will *not* miss the Super Bowl, Wimbledon, the World Cup, the Olympics, etc. Each one of these words has huge concepts attached to them - the concepts of *victory, achievement, fame, wealth and glamour.*

If you use logic, you will find that most sports are about a ball that is kicked, thrown, carried and/or hit. The world does *not* see it that way. It sees these sports as a matter of *competition, victory, achievement, fame, glamour and wealth.*

By now, you may understand the virtual, conceptual nature of these events. However, you may say these are occasional events in your life. Well, take a close look at the usual activities of your daily life and you realize that most human activities are in the *domain* of the conceptual, virtual world.

Here are some examples: (*Let me make it very clear that I am making these observations using simple logic. I am not criticizing, putting down or making fun of any of these concepts. Of course, you don't have to agree with me.*)

The Internet, TV, newspapers and magazines obviously take you into the virtual, conceptual world. Many people start their day reading a newspaper or watching a morning show on TV. They glance through magazines or surf the Internet during the day. In the evening, they usually watch TV or surf the

Internet. Most are hooked on TV or the Internet for hours every day.

It's interesting to see some older people complain about young people wasting too much time on the Internet, playing video games or texting. Meanwhile, they waste their time reading newspapers, watching TV and talking about politics or religion.

Everything you read in newspapers, magazines and books or watch on TV and the Internet is conceptual and virtual, isn't it?

Everything in movies, stage shows, museums and art galleries is conceptual, isn't it? All pictures, paintings and statues are obviously conceptual.

All knowledge, whether history, mathematics, science, arts, geography or business is virtual and conceptual, isn't it? In this way, all of the educational system is conceptual.

Language itself is conceptual. Observe how every word carries a concept with it, as we observed earlier in the book.

How about political and social systems? All are conceptual.

How about religious establishments? Those are all conceptual as well.

How about cultures, traditions and values? Those are all conceptual.

In reality, you see mountains, land, buildings, roads, trees, animals, sky, clouds and water. However, on a map you see continents, countries, states, provinces and cities - all conceptual.

How about marriage, romance, engagement, divorce? All are concepts, aren't they?

How about time? Seconds, minutes, hours, days, weeks, months and years. All conceptual. Different cultures have created different calendars.

How about national, religious and cultural holidays? All conceptual.

There are concepts attached to gold, platinum, jewels and diamonds. In fact, these are simply metals and rocks, but there are huge concepts attached to them.

How about money? This concept is so overwhelming that no one ever thinks of it as conceptual.

The Concept Of Money

Almost everyone is in the grip of the concept of money and the economy. For most people, it also creates a lot of worries.

What is the economy? It's a concept isn't it? You cannot see the economy. You see currency, which itself is a concept. One Dollar, ten Euros, five Yen, a hundred Pesos, fifty Rupees, etc.

If you give a hundred dollar bill to a one -year - old, she will probably put it in her mouth, chew on it or rip it apart. Why? Because she still has *not* acquired the concept of money. However, give the same hundred dollar bill to her when she is a teenager and she will be thrilled to have it. Why? Because, by now she has acquired the concept of money. In reality, it is a piece of paper, but of course, there is a concept attached to it.

Everyone wants to make money. Money itself is a concept, but people don't think of it that way. To them, money is real. *"You can't do anything without money,"* you may argue, but that still does not make it real. *It may be necessary to some extent, but it is not real. To live in the conceptual world, you need money, but it still does not make it real.*

95

If you look deeper, you'll find that money is a way for humans to *trade* with each other. Not too long ago, people also used chickens, eggs, rice, etc. to purchase services from each other.

Animals don't do any trading. Obviously, humans developed the *concept of trading.* The concept of trading came into being when humans started living in communities. For example, "I can exchange my eggs for your wheat." Initially, it served a purpose, but then it took over the human race. The concept of precious metals and money came into being. The more money (or precious metals) they had, the more they could buy. Initially, they bought things of necessity: food items, clothes, houses... But this was not enough. They wanted to acquire more and more. Why? Because society also created other concepts: The concepts of prestige, fame, glamour, enjoyment, entertainment, vacations and power. The more money you have, the more powerful, the more famous and the more prestigious you are. You can also have a high profile life-style.

With money, you can purchase various conceptual objects: the car of your dreams, your dream home, your dream vacation, etc. Money is *no* longer just a means to buy the things of basic necessities. It is often used to *enhance* your ego, which is part of the Acquired Self.

These days, "wanting more" is the driving force behind the concept of money. There is never enough of it when you are in the grip of "wanting more." Even a *billionaire* wants to get more!

What's Wrong With Concepts?

There is nothing *inherently* wrong with concepts. It is only when they are not treated as concepts, but as reality, that they become *problematic* and create stress for you and others.

Use logic and you'll realize that *concepts are not reality and reality is not conceptual...* But all humanity is lost in concepts and believes in them as if they were absolute truth. People get attached to concepts. They either love them (positive attachment) or hate them (negative attachment). Then, actions arise out of these attachments. Actions arising out of concepts create a huge amount of stress for you as well as everyone else.

Concepts also divide humans into groups. Each group believes their own concepts to be true. This obviously creates *conflict*. One group sees the other group as a *threat* to their collective belief system, which creates collective fear. This often leads to violence verbal as well as physical and can even lead to battles and wars.

5. Utilize Your Acquired Self To Function In The World

The collective *conceptual* world, which we call the world, downloads a *conceptual* world into everyone's head, which is their Acquired Self. The two worlds are *extensions* of each other and *feed* each other. Basically, it is one big *conceptual* world.

Do not start to hate your Acquired Self. In fact, your Acquired Self has its relative significance. It is your <u>tool</u> to function in the conceptual world, but obviously it is *not* you. The problem arises when you mistakenly believe your Acquired Self *is* you and you lose your true identity. Then, you are <u>enslaved</u> by your Acquired Self, which creates tons of stress for you and others. On the other hand, you need to *rise* above it and be its <u>master</u>, not its <u>slave</u>.

While interacting in the conceptual world, utilize your Acquired Self, but don't get overtaken by it. As soon as you don't need the assistance of your Acquired Self, switch gears and shift your attention to the Now.

6. Stress Free Living

With few exceptions, everyone is consumed by the *conceptual* world in their head, their Acquired Self and the collective, *conceptual* world, which we call the world.

As we observed, the conceptual world is full of stress. That's why people are so stressed out. They don't see any way out. They often *rationalize* their stressful living with statements such as "Oh, stress is part of life. There's nothing you can do about it." Then, they seek refuge in *escapes,* such as drugs, alcohol, partying, vacationing, gambling, etc, which provide only temporary relief and actually add more stress in the long run.

Once you *clearly* realize the *conceptual* nature of the "I" and the *conceptual* nature of the world, you are *free* of them. With this *mental* shift, a profound wisdom sinks in and your life becomes *stress free* automatically.

For example, you realize money is a concept. It helps you earn a living in the conceptual world, that's all! You earn money to meet the basic *necessities* of life such as food, shelter, clothing, transportation, etc. However, you clearly see the difference between "necessities" and "wanting." You realize it is the Acquired Self that has a never-ending list of "wanting," which is the basis of greed and lack of contentment.

You also clearly see how the Acquired Self *boosts* up its ego by pursuing certain respectable professions, by seeking fame, by living in a mansion, by acquiring certain possessions or by living a certain lifestyle. You also see the rat race everyone is in to make more and more money and how it creates a huge amount of stress in their life.

Once you are free of wanting, greed and ego, you are *content* with whatever job or business you are in, as long as it provides you with the income to make a basic living.

Once you are *not* in the rat race any longer, you have plenty of time to prepare your meals. You can actually sit down and enjoy your meal.

When you are not attached to your house, possessions or lifestyle, you are not worried about losing them.

Once you are free of your ego, the need for praise and validation evaporates. The emotional drama of respect and insults comes to an end.

In the grip of the conceptual world, a lot of people end up doing shady stuff to make more money. Then, they are *afraid* of being caught. Once you are free of greed, you obviously don't get into illegal practices to make more money. Then, you're *not* afraid of being caught, because you're not doing any shady stuff.

In addition, you don't seek your *identity* through your profession, certain title or position. Then, you *don't* have thoughts about losing them and worries remain miles away.

As a student or parent of a student, you are no longer in a race to go to a prestigious university. As a student, you figure out what you're good at and pursue that particular field. It may or may not bring you a lot of money, but you are fine with this, because you are free of your Acquired Self and therefore, free of wanting, greed and ego. In this way, you don't have to go through tremendous worries such as "What if I don't get accepted at a prestigious university?"

You realize <u>rules are concepts</u>, but you also acknowledge their functional value. Therefore, you *follow* traffic rules, you *follow* campus rules, you *pay* your income tax and you *follow* the rules of your profession or business. In this way, you become a perfect law-abiding citizen. You have *nothing* to hide. Then, you have *no* fear of being caught.

Once you realize all rules are concepts, you follow them yourself, but don't judge others if they don't. In this way, you don't fume over "those bad people", who don't follow the rules on the freeways, in ~~the~~ offices, in ~~the~~ political, religious and cultural parties etc.

Once you realize *expectations* and *morality* arise out of the "book of role descriptions," written by your society: "how everyone should and shouldn't behave," you automatically stop having expectations. Consequently, you have no disappointments, annoyances and anger.

In addition, you automatically stop judging all of "those immoral, bad people." You do your role by the book, but don't judge others. In this way, you stay free of a lot of frustrations and anger.

You realize political systems and parties are conceptual. Then you don't get into heated arguments with others, over the political issues. You don't get angry by watching TV shows or reading newspapers. You realize you can *impact* your virtual political system by casting your vote every few years and that's all. You don't keep fuming over the results of elections, in case your party did not win.

You realize marriage is a concept, but you also realize its functional value and *follow* it as a part of living in a society. Free of your Acquired Self, you don't get into the mess of extra-marital affairs, which is the activity of the Acquired Self to enhance its ego or to escape from emotional pains. Obviously, if you don't have any affairs, you don't worry about being caught.

You realize beauty is a concept. Consequently, you *don't* worry if you lose a few hairs, if your hair start turning grey or if a wrinkle or a pimple appears on your face. You don't dye your hair, apply wrinkle cream or see a plastic surgeon. All the *worries* about side effects of these dyes and creams, the high cost of plastic surgery and its possible side effects automatically do not arise.

You recognize the conceptual nature of all sports, television shows and stocks. Then, you *don't* worry about the loss of your team, the fate of your favorite TV show or the performance of your stocks.

You realize that Internet, TV, newspapers and magazines keep you *trapped* in the conceptual world. Automatically, you don't spend much time on these activities. Then, you don't hear sensational, horrifying and dreadful news and stay free of unnecessary fear.

You realize "special days" do not exist in the Real, but only in the conceptual world. Then you don't have *expectations* from others to do certain things on certain special days, such as birthdays, anniversaries, religious and national holidays. No expectations mean no disappointments, if someone does not live up to your expectations. You also become free of self-criticism and guilt.

You realize your present lifespan, in Reality, is a line between birth and death. It is your society's Collective Acquired Self that *artificially* divides this line into *segments* such as childhood, youth, middle age and old age. Then you are free of the *anguish* once you turn 40.

Once you clearly see the virtual nature of the past and the future, you don't *fume* over the painful memories or *miss* the good old times or *worry* about the future. You also become free of the collective emotional pains of your group, race or nation, due to history being kept alive. At the same time, you don't worry about the collective future of your group, race, nation or the entire human race. In stead, you keep your attention in the Now: what is in front of you, what you sense with your *five* senses.

Once you realize that concepts divide humans into political, social, cultural and religious groups and create conflict, you automatically are not *emotionally* attached to them. In this way, you become free of the collective "hate and revenge" that *plagues* the majority of the human world.

In short, you *minimize* your interactions in the conceptual world to bare <u>necessities</u>. In this way, you *free* up a lot of time to spend in the Real world, the Now, where there are no worries, frustrations, anger, regrets, hate, jealousy, sadness or worthlessness. And it is *not* a boring life. Quite the opposite! Once you are in touch with the Now, you tap into an *immense* source of <u>joy</u> and <u>inner peace</u>. Then, you have no need to seek thrill, excitement and entertainment.

That's how you live a life that is *joyful*, *peaceful* and completely *free* of emotional stress.

To learn more about stress management, please refer to my book, "Stress Cure Now."

Chapter 16

True Enlightenment Versus Conceptual Enlightenment

When a person frees himself from his Acquired Self during his lifetime, he lives a stress-free life. When such a truly enlightened person dies, his <u>untarnished</u> REAL Self simply <u>assimilates</u> back into the vastness of the REAL GOD.

An untarnished REAL Self has no emotions, but an immense sense of inner peace. That's how a truly enlightened person lives after he dies: Pure consciousness with a sense of immense inner peace: eternal peace or peace of REAL GOD.

It is important to understand what I mean by a *truly* enlightened person, as there is a lot of confusion in this regard. There are a lot of persons who consider themselves to be enlightened, while they stay in the grip of their *noble* concepts and continue to *judge* and *experience* emotions. In fact they are still in the prison of their Acquired Self. All they have done is *replace* some of their so-called bad concepts with the so called good or noble concepts. It is like <u>rearranging</u> the contents of a room. They don't realize that room is the problem. True freedom is to step outside the room. True enlightenment is to be completely free of your Acquired Self; which means total freedom from <u>all</u> concepts, conceptual thoughts, judging and triggered emotions - bad as well as good.

Chapter **17**

Meditation

Meditation is a great way to shift your attention from the Acquired Self into the NOW.

Every day, spare at least 15 minutes in the morning and 15 minutes in the evening to do some meditation. Morning meditation prepares you to start your day with a relaxed mind. Evening meditation helps you to wash away all the emotional burdens you may have collected during the day. It also prepares you for a restful sleep.

The Art of Meditation

You can do meditation in a sitting position or a lying down position: whatever is comfortable for you. For most people, sitting in a chair works well. If you are more flexible, then you can sit on a mat in a more traditional lotus or half lotus position with your legs crisscross.

There are several types of meditation. You can do them together in sequence or separately.

Be in a quiet area away from phones and other noises. No music either. Sit or lay comfortably. Close your eyes.

Body Meditation

Pay attention to your body parts, starting with your feet. Feel the weight, pressure and sensation in your feet. Now move your attention to your legs, knees, thighs and pelvic area. Mentally feel each area for a minute or two. Then move onto the lower back, middle back, and upper back. Stretch your entire back with your imagination. Then focus on your neck and skull. Then bring your attention to your face. Soften the muscles and come down to the neck, arms, chest and abdomen, spending few minutes at each area, mentally feeling and softening each area.

Breathing Meditation

Bring your attention to your breathing. Observe how your chest expands with each inhalation and retracts with each exhalation. Just feel the movement of your chest.

No thinking, but just pay attention to your breath and the energy flowing inside your body. If your mind runs away with some thought, do not get upset. As soon as you realize that your attention was distracted, bring it back to the movement of your chest with each breath. Your chest movement becomes the anchor of your attention.

Initially, you will find that your mind is as busy as a bee, but gradually, it starts to calm down. You gradually start to feel a pleasant *spacious* feeling in your chest. You may also see some shapes, usually purple colored, in front of your closed eyes. Don't get involved. Keep your attention on your chest movements and *spacious* feeling in your chest. Every now and then you feel intense vibrant sensations running throughout your body. This is life energy.

Continue to be the observer, paying attention to all that's happening in your body. You may be amazed to discover the *energy*, *joy* and *peace* that you never experienced before.

Walking Meditation

As you get tired of sitting, get up and start walking. Pay attention to each step. Realize how the right arm and left leg move forward and backward together (and the left arm and right leg move forward and backward together).

To keep it simple, just pay attention to one set of arm and leg. I use the right arm and left leg. Also, pay attention to your breathing, the space in which your body is moving forward. You can sense the walls of the corridor moving backward, if you are walking in a corridor, of course.

Meditation All the Time

Keep your mind where your body is. Then you meditate while carrying on your daily activities. While driving, pay attention to space and everything in it: electricity poles, traffic, trees, birds, sky, clouds, etc. In the parking lot, pay attention to space and everything in it: other cars, curbs, concrete, signs, etc. In your office, be aware of space and everything in it: desk, computer, chair, walls, people, etc. In the grocery store, be aware of space and everything in it: the aisles, items on the shelf, people, carts, lines, clerks, machines, etc. In a restaurant, pay attention to space and everything in it: chairs, tables, items on the table including your food, walls, people, etc.

Every now and then, also pay attention to your breath. Feel how with each inhalation, energy rises from the base of your spine to the top of your spine and then into your head. With each exhalation, energy flows down from your head into your chest and abdomen. You may be sitting alone in a restaurant or driving your car and feeling peaceful and joyful with this energy flowing up and down your body. It is such a great feeling. Words cannot describe it. You have to experience it yourself.

Imagine, next time you are in a traffic jam or in a line at the airport or grocery store, you will be joyful and peaceful in your meditative state, instead of being stressed out. This is the key to stress-free living.

It is relatively easy to stay in the meditative state while you are alone, even if you are in a social setting, such as eating alone at a restaurant or waiting in a line. But it is quite challenging when you are in company and you have to participate in a conversation. As soon as you engage in conversation, you easily get taken over by your Acquired Self. Then, you are not in the Now.

However, you can master the art of paying attention to your surroundings, the space around you, and carry on a conversation. It is useful to remember to come to a *full stop* after expressing your opinion and to know that it is your opinion, not the ultimate truth. You don't need to defend it. Every now and then, you will be taken over by your Acquired Self, but soon you will realize it and get out of its grip.

Meditation Can Enlighten You

After a few sessions of meditation, you may start to re-experience your past experiences. This time, see them as an observer. See how your Acquired Self and Acquired Selves of others were at each other's throats in those experiences. Do not judge. Just observe.

Then, you may have a new realization about your past experiences. For example, in the past, you got upset with your brother, a friend or a parent who let you down. They did not behave in the manner that your Acquired Self wanted. You carry all of that psychological pain with you all the time. Imagine over your lifetime, how many times others, especially the one you had expectations from, let you down and caused emotional pains. Imagine the amount of pain you are carrying.

Can you fully realize that your relatives or friends did not meet the expectations of your Acquired Self? It's your Acquired Self that created the emotional drama. Only once you fully realize it, can you let go of it. You will truly be amazed how transforming this experience can be. You feel a huge weight lift off your chest. This is true forgiveness with tremendous healing power.

Compare it to the usual concept of forgiveness: You forgive someone because you're a better person or you must forgive, otherwise you will be punished. This actually nourishes your Acquired Self and that's why it has no real healing potential.

Chapter **18**

Dealing with Stressful Situations

Most people stay in the grip of their Acquired Self, which torments them constantly, creating inner stress even when there is no *stressful situation*.

In life, sooner or later, one faces a stressful situation, which we can call **outer stress**. Already up to their neck due to ongoing **inner stress**, most people overreact to the outer stressful situation, creating more stress for themselves and for others.

For example, you may call for tech support help for your computer and get a representative who speaks with a foreign accent. This tech support helper may very well be physically sitting in an office in a foreign country. If you (actually your Acquired Self) already dislike foreigners for one reason or other, you have little patience with this person on the other side of the phone, who with her little training tries to help you. You may find yourself bursting into a *rage* at her, which of course makes matters worse. The tech support helper may hang up on you or may be so terrified by your temper, that she becomes even less effective in solving your problem. Later, you may tell your version of the story to your friends who probably agree with your action and this validation further strengthens your Acquired Self. While telling the story, you experience *hate* and *anger* again and actually cause harm to your own health. In addition, you add to the emotional burden you are already carrying.

So What's the Solution?

There is another way to handle stressful situations, which actually turns out to be more effective in solving the problem and does not produce stress for you or the other person.

In the example mentioned above, someone who already has some insight into his Acquired Self may see the "Monster" of *prejudice* and *hate* rising inside him before he starts to yell. May be he realizes in the middle of his yelling, that it is his "Monster" who has taken over. Seeing the "Monster" is enough. As soon as you can see it, it does not hold control over you. Free of the "Monster," this person clearly sees what's happening. He may find himself saying, "Sorry, it's nothing personal, but I'm just tired of waiting such a long time on the phone, but I do appreciate you trying to help me." The person on the other side may go the extra mile and being free of stress, will be more capable of finding the solution.

When you're out of the grip of your Monstrous Acquired Self, you actually communicate in a much more effective manner and get much better results. When you are not emotionally charged, you can actually think clearly and say exactly what the problem is. Chances are that you or your helper will be able to find the answer.

Once you are free of your Acquired Self, your inner stress dissipates and you don't overreact to stressful situations.

Often, your Acquired Self takes you back in its prison before you know it. You start to overreact to a situation, but soon you realize that your Monster took you over and caused you to act the way you did. This realization has a transforming effect. You may find yourself apologizing to your spouse, your child or your employee, much to their surprise. Each time you see the Monster in action, even if you see it after the fact, it loosens its grip on you.

When you are not in the grip of your Acquired Self, you also start to live in a practical way, which tremendously reduces the magnitude of your outer stress. You are able to look at any stressful situation with logic, without any emotional overreaction.

For example, you lose your job for one reason or another and face a financial situation. If you already live in a practical way, chances are that you won't have heavy debts. You will be free of the heavy monthly expenses that most people incur these days. You further reduce your expenses as your income drops. Thinking logically, you look at your options and take action if necessary.

Most Situations are Actually Not Stressful at All!

Use logic and you will see that all stress comes from the conceptual world in your head, your Acquired Self. When you are consumed by the conceptual world, you constantly face stressful situations. On the other hand, when you rise above the conceptual world, the stressful situation is not stressful any longer.

Example:

Traffic jams and all of the resulting stress is a product of the civilized, conceptual world, isn't it? Most people experience this stress every day. Is it possible not to experience the stress of heavy traffic? In the grip of the conceptual world in your head, (which is your Acquired Self), you say, "No. The stress due to traffic is part of life and you have to live with this stress." This thinking gives rise to an underlying emotion of *helplessness*. However, once you are free of the conceptual world in your head, your Acquired Self, you no longer experience the stress due to traffic jams.

<u>Example:</u>

A man in the total grip of his Acquired Self gets into a traffic jam while driving to the airport. His Acquired Self torments him with the fear of missing the flight and all the consequences that may happen if he misses the flight. He soon starts blaming his wife for being late. Of course, his wife's Acquired Self strikes back with some defensive comment, "It's all your fault and you're blaming me? How dare you?!! You always do that. I'm sick of your behavior." This war between the two monsters goes on, verbally or silently, until they arrive at the airport. Of course, both are totally stressed out and if anything else goes wrong, he will get into a rage and create a scene.

Now consider another driver, who has some freedom from his Acquired Self. He sees his Monster of fear and anger rising, but will not get lost in its grip. He uses logic and looks at his choices. "I cannot leave this situation, I cannot change this situation, so I should better accept it the way it is, drive carefully and not get in an accident." If he also remembers to "keep your mind where your body is," he will pay attention to his surroundings, space and everything in it. He will also pay attention to his breathing and feel the energy flowing in his body. This driver arrives at the airport at the same time as the first driver, but without any stress whatsoever. Actually, he will be in a meditative state, full of peace, joy and energy.

In the very same situation, one person collected and distributed a lot stress. In contrast, the other person dealt with it without any stress.

Therefore, it is very important for you to be free of your Acquired Self even when there are no stressful situations. And put *meditation at all times* into practice. Then, at the time of "stressful situations," you will not overreact. You will deal with the situation while remaining peaceful, joyful and full of energy. Only then, you realize that most situations are not stressful at all.

Practical Steps to Handle a Stressful Situation

Next time you're faced with a stressful situation, try to follow these steps. Be still and shift your attention into the Now. Observe your field of awareness by looking, hearing, smelling, touching and tasting. Pay attention to your breathing. Count your breaths.

Then, you will be able to observe your Acquired Self reacting to the situation. Be aware of the thoughts running through your head: *What if, What may*, etc.; Realize these are just thoughts, that's all. What they imply is not real, because it is not happening at this very moment. Then see what your options are. Ask yourself:

1. Is there a need for action?

Often there is *no* need for action. For example, you're driving on the freeway and someone cuts right in front of you, even without turning his car indicator light on. If you are in the grip of your Acquired Self, you may react almost instantaneously, as a knee jerk reflex. You may honk at the other driver, give him a finger, shout some curse words, etc.; Your Monster of *competition* and *self-righteousness* is in full action. In a fast mode, it is thinking like this: "That guy got ahead. I got behind. He won and I lost. He is a bad guy who didn't follow the rules." Your Monster decides to fight back and takes an action that creates a huge amount of stress for you as well as the other driver, who may decide to fight back. This is the basis of *road rage*.

However, if you are free from your Acquired Self, you clearly see it's the other driver's monster in action. You see how it invites your Monster to engage. You simply keep driving as if nothing happened. No stress for you and no stress for the other driver. You did not take any action at all and effectively prevented a stressful situation.

2. Sometimes you need to take action:

There are occasions when action may be necessary and you can take action to change the situation.

For example:

- You have medical problems from being overweight. You can change your eating habits.

- You are about to be robbed. You can run.

- You don't like your long work hours and you are self-employed. You can take action by cutting your hours. Of course, this may result in a reduction in your income.

- Your receptionist is rude and unprofessional to your clients and does not change her behavior despite several warnings from you. You can take action and terminate her.

- Your boss or coworkers are too mean to you. You can point out to them, as well as the authorities such as the personnel department. If things do not change, you may decide to look for another job.

While you live in the Now the solution to the situation will arise inside you. It will be without any *fear, anger, revenge, bitterness, self-righteousness* or *greed*. In your heart, you will know it is the right thing to do. **In addition, you will not look for certain results.** You will not be attached to the results at all.

On the other hand, actions that arise out of your Acquired Self are tainted by your Acquired Self and are filled with *anger, hate, jealousy, judgment, greed, self-fulfillment* or *fear*. Often, these actions are attached to certain results. For example, I often hear my patients ask, "If I follow what you are telling me, will I lose 15 pounds in two months and will I be able to prevent diabetes?" I tell them, "Just take action. Simply change your eating habits and that's all. Don't be attached to the results."

116

3. Sometimes you cannot take any action.

In many situations, there is no action that you can take, just as we saw in the example of the traffic jam on the way to the airport. If you cannot take any action, simply realize that. Stay in the Now, and continue to live your life. If you are totally in the Now, there will be no psychological stress for you. While there may be physical distress, there will be no psychological stress. In this way, you prevent any more emotional stains on your REAL Self.

Chapter **19**

The Choice is Yours

Now you understand that you have the great opportunity in this lifespan to wake up. Free yourself from the virtual world in your head as your Acquired Self, as well as the collective virtual human world. Only then you can be truly stress-free in this life, and the life after death.

The choice is yours! This is the most important choice in your life. Unfortunately, most people are not even aware of this choice. Stuck in the grip of their Acquired Self, they are unaware of this choice.

After reading this book, you clearly understand that you are the one who is ultimately in the driver's seat. This is true empowerment and does not arise out of insecurity. You can choose *not to be* in the virtual world of your Acquired Self. Instead, you choose to live in the Real Now: REAL GOD.

Therefore, at any given moment, ask yourself, "Am I in the grip of the Acquired Self? Am I lost in my *thoughts, concepts, emotions, beliefs, past* and *future*?" The moment you realize that, you have been hijacked by the Acquired Self, you actually are no longer in its total grip. It is only when you are *not* even aware that you are lost in the Acquired Self that you continue to experience emotional stress.

Awareness is the key. To be aware that you are taken over by the Acquired Self will release you from its prison immediately.

Freed from the Acquired Self, you park your attention into the Now by using your *five senses.* Then, you become aware of the *space, silence* and *stillness* in which every thing is. In the *bliss of Now,* you choose to live. You choose to be in touch with your *inner peace and joy.* You choose to be in touch with REAL GOD. This is the ultimate choice! Don't ever forget it.

Wake up and start to implement this very important choice in your life right now, while you can, as death can happen at any moment.

Real Questions, Real Answers

Q: If I am not my Acquired Self, then Who am I?

A: There is a Real Self that every living form is born with. You are your Real self. This self is Real hence, it needs no description. You can experience it right now. It is the Real self that sees, hears, smells, tastes and touches. It is the awareness, the consciousness, the soul. You are born with it. You could call it the Real "I".

Q: Why Do I have an Acquired Self? I hate it.

A: The Acquired Self is a tool, which helps you to function in the civilized world. You acquire it as you grow up in a society. In other words, your society downloads it into your mind. This leads to the conditioning of the mind.

As you grow up in a society, you (your REAL Self) gets attached to this Acquired Self. You start to believe this is who you are. This is how the Acquired Self imprisons you. Then it controls your thoughts, emotions and actions and creates a lot of emotional stress for you and the others around you.

If you start to hate your Acquired Self, you simply create a negative attachment. You still remain attached to it. The key is to separate your self from it through wisdom. Then you utilize it when you need it otherwise you put it to rest. In this way, your Acquired Self has no control over you. This leads to stress-free living.

Q: I am trying to live in the present moment but it is so hard. What can I do to achieve this goal?

A: People often say, "I want to live in the present moment." Ironically the very next moment they will be talking about something far away from the present moment. Silly, isn't it!

You want to live in the present moment but you don't. You try to live in the present moment but you keep finding yourself far way from the present moment. After a while, you may get frustrated trying to live in the "Now." "It is so hard," says an inner voice. "But I should keep trying and one day, I will get there." You stay determined, not to give up so easily. "Although it is hard, but I will keep trying to live in the Now. Hopefully one day, I will get there."

Use logic and see under the surface. You will find out there is a virtual "I" who has a "desire" to "live in the Now" which obviously becomes a concept. In other words, the virtual "I" wants to achieve something because it sounds like a good concept.

Who is this "I." It is your Acquired Self, isn't it. Acquired self consists of ideas, concepts, knowledge, past and future etc. And it loves to keep adding concepts to itself. Your Acquired Self has acquired one more concept, "the concept of living in the Now". Perhaps you read it in a book or heard it from someone. Acquired self is also full of "wanting", "having goals". That's how it has been conditioned right from childhood. When it does not get what it wants, it gets *disheartened* and *frustrated*. It is also conditioned never to give up, so, it keeps trying. From its experience, it has learnt that if it keeps trying, one day it may achieve its goal. In short, your Acquired Self, which is a *phantom*, is trying to achieve a *concept,* which is also a *phantom*.

It is interesting to observe that your Acquired Self has a *goal* to achieve, which obviously creates future. And the goal is to "live in the Now." How ironic! You never find "Now" in the future.

Observe little babies. You will see that they truly live in the "Now," without any effort. They obviously don't have the concept of living in the "Now" because they haven't read a book about it or heard it from any one. They don't even understand language, which itself is conceptual. They have no concepts, no knowledge, no past and no future. *That's why they live in the "Now" without trying to live in the "Now."* They haven't acquired the Acquired Self yet.

Therefore, what you need to do is to be free of your Acquired Self. Once free of the Acquired Self, automatically you live in the Now, without any effort. But DO NOT make a concept out of it.

"Now" is not a concept. It is REAL. It cannot be described. *The moment you start describing "Now" you are not in the "Now."* Because, all language is conceptual. *Concept and reality are mutually exclusive.* Reality is not a concept and concept is never real. So, get out of concepts, get out of your busy mind, your Acquired self. Then you are automatically in the "Now". Don't try to understand or conceptualize " Now". That's all!

How do you get freedom from your Acquired self? By understanding your Acquired self, by realizing that your Acquired self is not who you truly are! Acquired self consists of ideas, concepts, past, future etc. Basically all of these are bundles of thoughts and emotions. So each time, you find yourself in the grip of thoughts, treat them simply as thoughts, no more. Whatever thoughts imply is unreal and conceptual. *So don't believe in your thoughts.* That's how you free yourself from thoughts, from your busy mind.

You need to stay *alert* because thoughts will attack you again and again. They want to consume all your attention. Realize it is simply the conditioning of your mind. It is no ones' fault. But you don't need to stay in the prison of your

125

conditioned mind. Simple realization is enough! It liberates you from the conditioned mind.

From a practical stand, at any moment you need to keep asking your self two questions: "Is it happening right now, in real, not just in your head?" Almost always the answer will be: No, it is not happening at this moment. The next question you should ask is: "so what is happening right now, in reality? Then you look around, listen to, touch, smell or taste. Also be aware of *space*, *silence* and *stillness*. <u>This is the present moment. And you are already in it</u>.

It is the Acquired Self that diverts your attention from Now towards itself. Lost in the virtual land of the Acquired Self, you search for the Now. How absurd!

To live in society, however, you need to utilize your Acquired Self. So use it when it is needed. In this way, it serves you, instead of you becoming its slave. Here are some practical hints how you can limit the activity of your Acquired self.

Stop acquiring more ideas, concepts and knowledge, if it is not necessary for your every day, practical living, such as your job.

Whenever you are talking, you are using language, which is all Conceptual. Therefore, when you are in the grip of your conversation, you are not in the Now. Therefore, avoid chitchatting, unnecessary socializing and excessive interpreting. Keep your conversations brief and simple.

Don't try to analyze and interpret everything. It is your conditioned mind, your Acquired Self that loves to interpret, judge and label everything, based upon the information stored in it.

When you are watching T.V, reading a book, or newspaper, or surfing the Internet, you are not in the Now. Therefore, limit these activities as much as possible. Also be fully aware that all of these activities take you into virtual and conceptual world.

Whenever you are alone, get out of your head, use your five senses and live in the Now.

Q: I have no time. I feel so rushed all the time. I don't know where the time goes. I have been to "time management" seminars, but it did not work for me. It makes me more stressed out to know that I am unable to manage my time. I feel like a failure. Is there a real solution?

A: You are lost in your Acquired Self, isn't it! Your Acquired self has already tried the concept of "time management", but it did not work. Now it wants to acquire and try some other concept in the form of a new technique.

Pause for a moment. Use logic and see for yourself that you need to get to the root of the problem before you can find a real solution. Otherwise the solution would be superficial and will not work in the long term.

So, first of all you need to find out yourself where does your time go. You will find out that you are busy doing one activity after another. Some activities come in the form of responsibilities: To make a living, to take care of your loved ones, to go to school; some activities come from your social commitments and obligations, some activities are centered around entertainment, fun, happiness; some activities are for some social, religious or political cause and some activities are to just socialize. These activities may be physical or mental. Your Acquired self stays busy in these activities and then wonders where did the time go.

If activities use up all of your time, you have to ask what is the basis of these activities. At birth, you did not know any concept of responsibilities, commitments, hobbies, missions, entertainment, socialization etc. All of these concepts get downloaded into your Acquired self as you grow up in the human world. In the grip of the Acquired Self, you are not aware of the conceptual, virtual nature of the Acquired self. You are also not aware of the virtual, conceptual nature of the human world. That's why you keep doing what your Acquired self tells you to do.

The moment you realize the human world is not real, the tight rope of compulsion to do the activities loosens up. Then you decide, using logic, what activities are necessary and what are unnecessary. For example, necessary activities include making a living, taking care of your loved ones. You will find out a lot of activities are unnecessary. You do these unnecessary activities because your Acquired self wants you to do these activities to have fun and entertainment, to get praised by the others in your social, political, religious group or to or get sympathy and validation by telling your side of the story through chitchatting and gossiping.

The moment you take your attention away from the Acquired Self and put it into the Now, you feel an inner joy, which is of different quality as compared to the joy or happiness or entertainment of the human world. Then the neediness to get fun, happiness and entertainment goes away. With that, all of the activities to get fun, entertainment and happiness also die out. Once you realize all humans are like yourself in Nature, you become free of the religious, political and social divisions of the human world. Obviously you will no longer have any desire to be involved in these activities.

Can you see how your life gets simplified automatically, once you use logic and see clearly the virtual nature of your Acquired self and the human world. Then you carry on the necessary activities only. Obviously then you have ample time to stay in the Now and be joyful, peaceful from within, without any activities.

Q: Our marriage has fallen apart. We have raised wonderful children, but a lot of "bad" things happened between us. We don't comfort each other any longer. I feel so lonely and sad, and at times mad. Any guidance to deal with this emotional mess?

A: You are stuck in the past, aren't you? Now lets examine what is the past? Basically your past consists of *events* that your conditioned mind, Acquired Self, judged to be good or bad, according to the *concept* of *morality* you acquired from your society. Judging triggers emotions, good or bad, depending upon "how your mind judges the event." The event gets stored in your memory and becomes part of your past. The event is long gone, but your mind has preserved it as "My past." Every time your mind visits these events, you experience the associated emotion.
You feel *mad* when you think of the bad memories. And you feel *sad*, because you *miss* the good old days, "how things used to be." Your past not only carries bad memories, but also good memories. Bad memories make you mad or guilty, and good memories make you sad.

It is pretty clear that your past is *Virtual* at this time. Events were real when they happened, but now they are NOT happening any longer, except in your head, in the form of thoughts, mental pictures and associated emotions. This basic understanding will *automatically* loosen your tight attachment to those events.

Don't try to change your past. Don't try to figure out "why did it happen," why did it not happen," "why did someone say or do something." Simply realize what happened is *unreal* at this moment.

Keep shifting your attention away from those emotional thoughts and into the Real Now: what you see, hear, smell, taste and touch, without any interpretation. The moment your thoughts do not have your attention, they *die out* and with that, their associated emotion, such as anger, guilt or sadness, goes away.

Also, realize that marriage is a concept, downloaded into your Acquired Self as a part of conditioning as you grow up in ~~the~~ society. The concept of marriage carries a number of sub-concepts: marriage is a union, marriage is to love each other till death sets you apart, marriage is to take care of each other, marriage is companionship, etc. Obviously, the concept of marriage gives rise to the expectation of companionship, love and care. If your spouse does not provide you with company, you feel lonely. If your spouse does not provide you with love, you feel hurt. If your spouse does not provide you with caring, you feel unworthy and may even become angry at his/her callous attitude.

Realize marriage is a concept, nothing more. It helps you to be able to function in the conceptual world, what we call the "world." That's all, nothing more. With this realization, your heavy emotional investment into the concept of marriage goes away and with that, all of the emotional drama arising out of expectations starts to subside. Then, you can decide to stay in the marriage or seek a divorce. It really does not matter.

Realize that you are born alone and you die alone. The source of true inner peace and joy reside inside you, not out there.

Q: I have not achieved much at my age. My parents are such high achievers. I feel like such a failure. Any guidance?

A: Pause. Shift your attention into the Real Now: what you see, hear, smell, taste and touch, without any interpretation. Then you can think logically.

Let me ask, "Who is this "I," who is comparing itself to its parents and judging itself to be a failure. It is your Acquired Self, isn't it! Concept of success and achievements is one of the principle concepts of the majority of Acquired Selves. In the collective conceptual world, the concept of success and achievements is also highly prevalent. Based on this concept, you and almost everyone else in the conceptual world, compares and judges each other. In addition, Acquired Self judges itself, even when no one else is around, which is the basis of self-criticism. Comparing and judging are the basic characteristics of the Acquired Self and the collective, conceptual, human world.

As long as you mistakenly think your Acquired Self is your identity, you will continue to stay trapped in the concepts, including the concept of success and failure. You will continue to compare and judge, which will continue to trigger the emotions of excitement when you are a success and worthlessness when you are a failure. Your friends in the conceptual world may try to boost up your low self-esteem when you are feeling worthless, by making you look at the bright side or point out how good you are in this or that. This kind of help may only *temporarily* help your emotion of worthlessness, but will keep you imprisoned in the castle of the Acquired Self.

Once you realize success and achievements are conceptual, virtual: there is nothing REAL about them. In the conceptual world, they may seem real to an Acquired self. But in Real, in Nature, they do not exist at all. With this realization, the compulsion to compare and judge automatically vanishes. And with that the sad emotion of worthlessness goes away. Then, you can acquire some skills to be able to make a basic living in the conceptual, human world.

Q: I will do because I have to do it. I don't have a choice.

A: When you feel you don't have a choice, it gives rise to a sense of *lack of freedom*, a *choking sensation*, and a sense of *imprisonment*. If it happens chronically or repeatedly, it creates a sense of *helplessness*, *hopelessness* and can even lead to *depression*. In addition, there is an underlying *desire* that you would rather be doing something else. Therefore, you do this enforced job half-heartedly and it clearly shows, which causes stress for your employer, parents, teachers or anyone else who is responsible for forcing you to do something against your choice or will. In this way, you create a lot of stress for yourself and the others involved in your life. Deep inside you also feel *unfairness* and want to *fight out* but somehow can't. This feeling gets buried in your pile of emotional burden but remains very much alive. At some later point in life, this smoldering emotional fire may cause you to *overreact* to some trivial thing, such as a comment from your spouse. And everyone wonders what happened?

Is there another way? A way that does not create stress for yourself and others? Let's take a deeper look. Who is this "I" who feels *compelled* to do something it really does not want to do. This "I" is your Acquired Self, isn't it? And you are doing things in the conceptual, human world. For example, you may have to work long hours, do your homework, go to a family get together, and walk through a museum with your parents or spouse etc. But you would rather spend time with your friends, go to a mall or have fun on the computer.

Your Acquired Self wants to do activities that it likes and does not want to do things it does not like. It boils down to your likes and dislikes or rather the likes and dislikes of your Acquired Self. As long as you are in the grip of your Acquired Self, you will continue to stay in the grip of your likes and dislikes. Naturally, when you are free of your Acquired Self, your likes and dislikes evaporate, automatically.

Q: How Can I control my busy mind? I understand it is my busy mind that is causing me a lot of stress. I have read a few books, tried various techniques, and attended several workshops. I get so frustrated that I cannot control my busy mind.

A: What is the basis of the busy mind? It is your Acquired Self, isn't it? The "virtual I" thinking, constantly based on the concepts and information stored in it. Obviously, the more information and concepts stored, the busier the mind. Then it get some more information on "how to calm your mind", some noble concepts and techniques. This obviously leads to even a busier mind, and all of the stress arising out of it, including the frustration that "I am unable to control my mind. I am some kind of a failure."

In addition to the concepts and information, the virtual "I" also creates mental pictures it calls "My memories'" or "My past." It often *stews* over the events, it has judged to be bad and *misses* the events it has judged to be good. For example: Why did someone insult me, I did not deserve it, why did my boyfriend cheat on me, why did my friend betray me, why didn't I say, "No", why did I do what I did, why was I so selfish, why didn't I take care of myself, I am so ashamed, I miss my children, I miss the great fun we had together, I miss my retreat buddies, I miss my mother, I miss my little town I grew up in etc. The virtual "I" also wants to learn from its past. Consequently, it gives rise to more thoughts it calls "My future". Here are some examples: "I wonder" "I wish" "what if", "what will I," "what will happen" etc. In this way, the mind stays busy, lost in the past and worrying about the future.

Obviously, your Acquired Self, the "virtual "I" is the basis of the busy mind. That's why you cannot be free of the busy mind, as long as you *misidentify* with your Acquired self to be who you are. In this way, you are *glued* to your Acquired self. Then it *sucks* up all of your attention. And you stay lost in the virtual world in your head that it creates.

135

Realize that your Acquired Self needs your attention to survive. Your attention is the "power line" for your busy mind. The moment you pull the plug out - take your attention away from the busy mind, it *dies* out momentarily. Then, you need to *park* your attention outside the domain of the Acquired Self or get sucked up again by your Acquired self, and the train of the busy mind will restart.

The Acquired Self is virtual. It does not exist in the Reality of the Real Now. Therefore, you park your attention into the Real Now: What you see, hear, smell, taste and touch: Also be aware of the space, silence and stillness.

Once you clearly see that Acquired Self is simply a tool to function in the virtual world created by humans, you are not attached to it any more. Then you are free of the mental compulsion to keep adding more and more information. Once you tap into the everlasting fountain of joy and peace inside you, you will lose the *desire* to seek pleasure, entertainment and happiness. You realize the virtual nature of money, fame and power and you don't pursue them anymore. You also realize the virtual nature of the past and the future. Automatically you don't dwell in them.

Also realize that your attention has been shifted into the direction of the Acquired self-your mind for a very long time. Therefore, your attention will keep going back to the Acquired Self for a while. Over and over again, you will realize that you are lost in your mind, that your Acquired Self had hijacked your attention. Obviously, you will shift your attention away from the busy mind and into the Real Now and your busy mind will die out due to the lack of its power supply: your attention.

In this way, the more and more you live in the Real Now, the less and less you live in the busy mind. Also the more you stay aware that you are *not* your Acquired Self, the less time you will spend in the virtual human world and more time in the Real world of Now: REAL GOD, which is all around you all the time. Consequently, you will *not* be adding more *ammunition* for the busy mind in the form of information, concepts and memories.

136

Q: I am out of a job, and this makes me very anxious. I am losing sleep over it. Any help!

A: Who is this "I" who is creating fearful thoughts and making you anxious? It is your Acquired Self, right. The virtual "I" that you *mistakenly* think you are, is creating a series of case scenarios of "what if", "what may" or "what will I." These thoughts provoke the emotion of fear, which manifests itself as anxiety, worrying and insomnia. As long as you continue to think that you are the virtual "I", you will continue to remain trapped in the thoughts and their triggered emotions. Lost in emotional thoughts, you will *not* find any logical answer. Any actions arising out of emotional thoughts often create more stress and usually are less effective in the long run.

Pause. Shift your attention away from your thoughts and into the Real Now: what you see, hear, smell, taste and touch, without any interpretation. The moment you take your attention away from the thoughts, they die out. With that their associated emotion dies out as well.

Then shift your attention into your chest and experience "the inner peace" that is always there. This is not a concept. Therefore, no words can describe it. But you can experience it anytime. This is the source of inner peace. Dwell in it.

Once you experience this "inner peace", you will be completely free of fear, and its manifestations of worries, anxiety and insomnia.

Once you are freed of the emotion of fear, you can think logically. Then you can think of taking some actions which will be non-emotional and often more effective. For example, you may decide to cut down your expenses till you find a job. Or you may be willing to accept less than the ideal job or any other practical solution to your financial situation. You also realize the conceptual nature of the world: the concept of success and failure, the concept of achievements, the concept of glory and fame, the concept of power, the concept of "being special", the concept of shame and embarrassment etc.

137

Then in the conceptual, human world, you can utilize your Acquired self to find a way to meet your basic necessities: food, shelter and clothing etc.

Q: I want to relieve peoples' emotional sufferings so desperately. Can technology help?

A: Obviously you are a *compassionate* person who wants to relieve peoples' emotional suffering. You are searching for ways to accomplish your mission. Have you wondered who is this 'I" who has a noble desire/mission to help people. It is your acquired self, isn't it?

Acquired self typically runs to find a solution when it recognizes a problem. In your case, you see the emotional suffering people go through and you want to find a solution. This is the typical *horizontal* approach in the virtual, conceptual, human world. For example, medical researchers have used technology to find treatment for depression, anxiety, attention deficit disorder and many other disorders. Basically they investigate the *mechanism* that leads to a specific emotional disorder. They may discover that a certain neurotransmitter is low or high in a certain emotional disorder. Then they use technology to alter the concentration of the *culprit* neurotransmitter and this relieves the symptom. The relief, however is *temporary* and also causes some additional symptoms as side effects.

Now, isn't it worthwhile to dig deeper and find out the *root cause* of the emotional pains: a *vertical* approach rather the typical *horizontal* approach mentioned above. So for a minute, do not run away from the problem by trying to find a quick, easy, convenient treatment. Instead, stay with the problem, dig deep *without* trying to find the solution and see what happens?

In order to find the real root cause of any problem, you have to be on the *neutral* grounds, without any emotional attachments to the problem. So you need to be free of your *compassionate* Acquired Self, isn't it? Then you may see the *root cause* of emotional pains in any person is actually their own Acquired Self. As long a person stays in the grip of their Acquired Self, they will continue to suffer from the emotional

139

pains. Therefore, the real freedom from the emotional sufferings lies in the freedom from the Acquired Self. With this clear observation, you obviously stop your search for any outside help in the form of techniques, technologies, or philosophies.

"The root cause of emotional sufferings lies inside you; hence the real solution must also reside inside you, without any outside help.

Q: I always see things as "black or white". My wife keeps suggesting, "I should see more gray". Who is right; my wife or I?

A: Who labels things as black or white. It's your Acquired Self, isn't it? You acquire concepts from your society as you grow up. Then you look at people, events, and things through the filters of these concepts, and judge them as good or bad. The more you are in the grip of the concepts, the more you will see things as "white or black". Your wife has acquired an additional concept that one should look at things *not* as black or white, but as gray. Her Acquired Self is expressing herself, that's all! Of course her advice has not worked on you. " Why should I look at things as gray whereas they are either black or white. If she doesn't see it that way, then it is her problem," says your Acquired Self as an inner voice. That's why your wife's advice has not worked on you. By the way, this is common advice people hear or read about and of course, it doesn't work. Now you understand why it does not work.

Now if you want to see things the way they really are, then you have to remove the goggles of your acquired concepts. Then, look at things. Only then you can see things afresh, without labeling them white, black or gray. Be free of the concepts and experience life the way it really is! This is the end of judging and labeling.

Q: I have difficulty "making a decision" and it bothers me. It also bothers my husband that I cannot make up my mind and creates a lot of stress for both of us. Isn't it wise to learn from the past and then decide? That's exactly what I try to do, but end up with a lot of indecisiveness.

A: Why does a person have difficulty in making decisions? Because she is afraid of making a wrong decision, isn't it? She uses her past and tries to figure out a path that will *not* be wrong and will *not* cause any harm to her or her loved ones. Right!

After a lot of thinking, she decides one way based upon her past experiences (and advice from others), but then she is still *not* sure if she made the right choice. So she starts thinking all over again. And this drama goes on and on in her head.

Thoughts such as" what if, what may, what will I" occupy her mind and torment her over and over again. That's why she cannot make up her mind. It drives everyone else crazy. The irony is that it makes her crazy as well. She gets frustrated and annoyed at her own self. "I am a grown up person and I should be able to take charge of my life", says her inner voice. But her inability to make decisions smacks her in the face. Then, she searches for rationalization and finds one that suits her psychological needs. "We all should learn from our past and that's exactly what I am doing".

Why is a person afraid of making a wrong decision? Only because she has a lot of knowledge in the form of her own experiences and others' experiences that she has heard or read about. These experiences of the others, she treats as if these are her own experiences. And she does not want to make the same mistake. Now her (and others) past experiences may not be exactly the same as she is faced with the situation now. But she has learnt from those experiences that one has to be very cautious about making decisions or "you may regret for the rest of your life." That's why she is having such a hard time making up her mind. She wants security but cannot find it. That's why she shakes and trembles inside. No one seems to understand and it bothers her even more.

Who is it, who wants to learn from the past? It is your Acquired Self, isn't it? As a part of growing up, you acquired the concept of "learning from the past". What is past? It is your memories. And who creates your memories? Your mind does! Who keeps these memories alive? Your mind does! Events happened years ago but in your mind, those are alive as if they are happening right now. Silly! But, not to your mind. Your mind treats these events as "part of me" because mind itself has created these memories. In this sense memories are delusional, not real. They appear real but they are not. Why? That is because they are not happening right now, in real, but only in your head.

Why mind creates these delusions, we fondly call memories. Obviously mind is dysfunctional. It is not just your mind, but it is everyone's mind. It is the human mind! And it is no one's fault. It is the side effect of the evolution of the human mind.

The law of nature is that every thing is in *flux.* Nothing is static. Events happen all the time. Every event has a "beginning and an ending, birth and death." But dysfunctional human mind does not like "ending or death," although it likes "beginning or birth". It wants to live forever. It does not like change and wants the *status quo* because that's how it feels *secure.* So it does not want any event to die. It is afraid of death. Therefore, it takes a mental picture of the event, attaches a story to it, judges it to be good or bad, based on the information already stored in it. The act of judging, triggers an emotion, positive or negative depending upon how it judged the event. Then the entire bundle of the *picture*, *story* and *emotion* is stored as a memory.

That's how mind continuously creates *past.* In addition to its own experiences, it gathers others' experiences that it reads or hears about, and stores them as well, in its memory box. The more information you have, the more full your memory box gets.

Your conditioned mind, your Acquired Self thinks thru the filters of your past. That's what is called "learning from the past." Obviously, it does not want any thing bad to ever happen to it again, based upon personal or others' experiences. It wants to make sure that its future will be *secure*.

In reality, future is nothing but a collection of thoughts, arising out of thoughts stored as memories. Future is virtual, phantom and unreal. It is a *concept*. But because everyone around you believes in this concept of "past and future", so do you. Everyone wants a prosperous, healthy secure future, as do you.

Perhaps, now you understand the whole dynamics of decision making, and why you, like many other people has such a hard time making decisions.

The solution obviously lies in liberating yourself from your Acquired Self: the creator of "the past and the future." Once you fully realize that there is no past and there is no future, you will have no need to be afraid of future; no need for compulsive thinking to avoid the wrong choices and no need to learn from the past.

Freed from the dark shadows of the past and the fearful monster of the future, you will use logic to make decisions and move on. Then you will realize that life is not about decisions but about living, right now. Life is a total waste if you compulsively try to shape up your virtual future or regret your delusional past.

Q: I don't have a job. My boyfriend dumped me. I feel like a loser. Life is so unfair to me? How can I be free of stress when I am drowning in it.

A: Pause! Shift your attention into the Now: What is in front of your eyes, not what is in your head. Then use logic.

Take a logical look at your life and everyone else's life around you. You will realize that we all live in a virtual, *conceptual world.* Collective conditioned human mind has created a world, which is built on concepts. Hence there is the concept of *success* and *failure, fairness* and *unfairness, love* and *hate, wealth* and *poverty, beauty* and *ugliness, boredom* and *entertainment, good* and *bad, virtue* and *vice, nonviolence* and *violence* etc.

All of these concepts get downloaded into your Acquired Self as a part of growing up. Society downloads all these concepts into you in order for you to be a good citizen of it. That's how it continues to perpetuate: through you and your offspring.

All of theses concepts started as a byproduct of human civilization, which itself started as a consequence of the evolution of the human mind.

Society starts conditioning your mind right from early childhood by downloading all sorts of concepts into you. To condition your mind, first of all it uses parents, then teachers, the whole education system, the books, the newspapers, the T.V., the internet, the businesses, the organizations, the corporations etc. You start believing in those concepts as everyone else around you does, as well. Like everyone else, you are *immersed* in the sea of conceptuality.

You develop an Acquired Self from conditioning from your society, and then it steals your identity. That's who you think you are. Then, you live through concepts, like everyone else does.

In this conceptual world, "having a job" is a sign of success and losing a job is a sign of failure. Having a boyfriend is a sign of success and *not* having a boyfriend is a sign of failure. You were told that if you live your life by the book you will be rewarded. But you find out that you are not being rewarded. Rather those who don't follow the rules are being rewarded. So you feel *cheated*. You think that life is *unfair* to you. Often you become *bitter* at life.

If you use logic, you will find out that *life* did not promise you any thing. It was *society* who promised you all sorts of things. It was society who told you to go to college to find financial security. It was society who conditioned you to pursue a romantic affair and promised you happiness in romance. Life has nothing to do with any of these concepts. *Life is real.* Concepts are *not* real. Life and concepts are two completely different landscapes.

Conceptual world brings you excitement and sadness, success and failure, financial security and financial insecurity, love and hatred etc. Life has absolutely nothing to do with these concepts. You were not born with these concepts. Society downloaded these concepts into you. So put blame where it belongs. Not at life but at society. *Don't confuse society with life.*

In the trap of the Acquired Self, you will continue to experience the drama of success and failure, romance and loneliness, wealth and poverty, fairness and fairness, vice and virtue, beauty and ugliness, good and bad, etc. It is in the nature of the conceptual world to perpetuate these concepts. Lost in the conceptual world, you will never find any real answers to your troubles.

Why *not* look at the source of your troubles and be free of it. But please remember not to start hating society as many individuals do when they go through the process of enlightenment. By hating, you develop negative attachment to society and remain trapped in your Acquired Self. You need to understand that society is a product of the evolution of the human mind. Therefore it is no one's fault. You simply see the conceptual world inside you and around you and rise above it. That's all!

Q: I have terrible headaches, constipation, a lot of gas rumbling in my stomach. I have been to several doctors. They ran several tests but all these tests turned out to be normal. What's wrong with me! I feel like I am falling apart. I am only 38 years old. I feel so annoyed, irritated and at times angry. My teenagers don't listen to me, and this drives me nuts. My husband does not listen to me either. We have been through family counseling. Each time we talk, we end up in a fight. I get so outraged. A doctor put me on a sedative and a mood stabilizer. But my symptoms continue! Any ideas.

A: I will presume that your medical doctors have looked into the possible medical reasons for your symptoms and did not find an answer. In that case, your symptoms are most likely a manifestation of stress, through the Mind-Body connection.

You feel annoyed, frustrated and at times angry. You have tried counseling, medications but your symptoms persists.

First of all pause! Shift your attention into the Now, what is in front of your eyes, without any interpretation: See what you see, hear what you hear, smell what you smell, feel what you touch and taste what you taste.

Use logic and look deeper. You feel frustrated, irritated and angry because your own children and husband do not listen to you, because you *expect* them to listen to you. After all, you are the mother and the wife. They are *supposed* to listen to you. Right! Why are they *supposed* to listen to you? Because they are your children, your husband. You expect certain behavior from your children and your husband, based upon the conditioning of your mind, your Acquired Self.

In the making of every ones' Acquired Self, society downloads software of "description of every one's behavior." It describes how a husband should and shouldn't behave, how a teenager should and shouldn't behave, how a mother should and shouldn't behave, how a wife should and shouldn't behave etc. Obviously these are concepts, developed by society and become part of one's Acquired Self.

When you are in the grip of your acquired self, you don't see them as concepts. You see them as some sort of truth. Then you expect others to behave according to these concepts and when they don't, you feel irritated and angry. Guess what! Others are judging you too according to the concepts in their Acquired Self. For example, your teenager probably thinks," I am a teenager and I have the right to ———— , but my parents do not understand. It makes me so mad." Or your husband may think, "I work so hard for this family, and all I hear is complaints. I deserve better, After all, I am the head of the family."

Everyone thinks through the concepts of, "how everyone should, shouldn't behave" and consequently, expects certain behavior from others. And when those expectations are not met, a person feels frustrated and angry. In addition to expectations, the Acquired Self always blames others for its frustration and anger and it wants to control their behavior according to its wishes.

As long as you are in the grip of your Acquired Self, you will continue to feel that you have certain rights and others should behave according to your wishes. In this mindset, you will continue to be frustrated and angry.

Only when you clearly see the psycho-drama created by the interaction of various Acquired Selves, that you will be able to free yourself from your own Acquired Self. And that's all what you need to do.

What happens when you are free from your Acquired Self? You don't have any expectations. End of expectations automatically bring an end to frustration and anger. Then you clearly see how things really are. You see that you cannot control others' behavior; neither is there any need to control others' behavior.

All you have to do is to control your own behavior by freeing yourself from your expectations arising out of your own conditioned mind.
Then, your Acquired Self does not engage with others' Acquired Selves and that is the end of any arguments.

It does not mean that you do not express your opinion or do not give your advice. You can point out your opinion. Because you are free of your Acquired Self, your opinion does not become you. You are very clear that it is only your opinion, not the absolute truth. Others may take your advice or may not take your advice. Either way it is fine.

The only exception is your young children. They need your advice. You may enforce your advice if you see your young children may get into danger without your advice.

Q: What if there is big disaster and I am unable to get my medicines. What will I do??? Shouldn't I be prepared and stockpile my medicines, just in case??

A: Let me point out," if the disaster is so big that it wipes out all the manufacturing plants, what makes you think that you will be alive. Chances are that you may not be alive. You may die with the stock pile of medicines by your side."

I understand if you disagree. As we are dealing with a situation that is hypothetical, all the answers will also be hypothetical. And there is no end to the hypothetical questions and answers.

Just feel how your body reacts when your mind is *immersed* in this kind of hypothetical situations. You may feel how your body gets tense, contracted and spastic. Feel the fear and anxiety this kind of thinking creates. Don't run away. Then take a few deep breaths, sit down, shift your attention into the Now, and use logic.

You will realize how thoughts create hypothetical, fearful situations and then try to find an answer. How silly! Why mind is so serious about finding the answers to a situation that does not even exist, because to it, the situation is no longer hypothetical. It starts to believe in it to be true, because it creates it. Obviously whatever mind creates, is real to mind.

In the grip of your conditioned mind (Acquired Self), you go one step further and start to *act* out according to your hypothetical answers. This creates strange, neurotic behavior, such as stock piling medicine. Your neurotic behavior will be pretty obvious to people around you. But in the grip of your thoughts, you will not see your behavior to be insane. You may even argue with others that they are wrong and you are right in doing what you are doing.

Use logic and you will realize that your mind has created a hypothetical situation and that's all. In reality it does not exist.

151

And why did your mind create a hypothetical situation? It is because it probably read in a newspaper or watched on the T.V. that "you ought to be prepared for disasters." That's how your conditioned mind works. It consists of various ideas, concepts and information and loves to continue to add to itself more and more ideas. It is hungry for more and more information which society readily provides to it. Most of the society establishments know that "Fear sells" and they thrive on it.

From the storehouse of information, contained in your Acquired Self, arise all sorts of thoughts, starting with phrases like, "what if, what may, what will I". In this way your conditioned mind, your Acquired Self, creates hypothetical fearful situations and then tries to find answers to feel *secure*. Acquired self is very *insecure*. Why? It does not want to die. So it keeps trying to figure out how it can control the possible hypothetical case scenarios, which may threaten its existence. Society gives it a fancy, intellectual phrase, "preparedness for disaster". Then it seems so reasonable. And your Acquired Self falls for it. Here is an interesting fact. Your Acquired Self is virtual. It does not even exist.

As long you are in the grip of your Acquired Self, you will continue to fall for hypothetical situations and continue to suffer from fear, anxiety and neurotic behavior generated from these thoughts.

Only when you are free from your Acquired Self, you start to see these hypothetical situations for what they really are: thoughts in your head and no more. Whatever they imply is *unreal* because it is not happening at this very moment.

Whatever happens in real, it happens in the present moment, and then you are able to deal with it because it is real. But you can never deal with a hypothetical situation, how prepared you may be.

With this insight, you don't believe in what these thoughts are saying. You don't obey the orders of "these fearful thoughts." That is the end of fear and anxiety and that is the end of neurotic behavior.

It does not mean that you should not use common sense. For example, it is okay to have a flashlight in your house in case electricity goes out at night. Take simple steps and then forget about hypothetical situations. In other words, don't dwell in hypothetical situations. Don't believe in your thoughts. If and when some disaster happens, it always happens in the present moment. And your common sense is always there to guide you. Your mind, on the other can never accurately predict how and when some disaster will unfold and therefore it can never be fully prepared, how hard it may try. That's all!

Q: I have "Anger issues". I know it is bad for me. I have tried to control it but no luck. Any advice!

It is encouraging that at least you realize that you have a problem in the form of anger. Many angry people don't even acknowledge that they have a problem.

Trying to control anger often does not work. It is like a patchwork and that's why it does not work in the long term. You may suppress your anger for a while but sooner or later it blasts into a volcanic eruption.

In order to deal with your anger, you need to dig deep and take a close look at the root cause of your anger. Only then you can get rid of it from the roots.

Why does a person get angry:

His expectations are not met
Or
He strongly feels that he is right and others are wrong.
Or
He is afraid inside.
Or
He feels insulted

Here are a few examples:

You may be mad at your wife because she did not listen to your advice and put you in a financial jam.
Or
Your boyfriend cheated on you.
Or
You feel that something is wrong with people these days. *They don't have work ethics or they don't care or they are morons, or greedy or selfish."*
You are angry with the president or governor or any other politician, or a political, religious or social group for doing things

154

that are simply wrong in your book. How could they ever do this and go to sleep at night".
Or
You are angry with your child because she disobeyed you, and got into trouble. You are afraid "what might have happened".
Or
While you were complaining about his services, the electrician told you to get lost and find someone else.

1. Expectations

One of the basic reasons for frustrations and anger is your expectations. You had certain expectations which did not come through and that's why you feel frustrated and angry.

What is the basis of expectations? What do we really mean by expectations? If you look at this question logically, you find that expectations really are a collection of ideas and concepts you acquire during your upbringing. These become part of your Acquired Self.

These concepts revolve around how others should and shouldn't behave towards you and how you should and shouldn't behave towards them. For example, you expect certain kinds of behavior from your spouse, parents, brothers, sisters, friends and colleagues and *vice versa*. In a way, society dictates how each of us should fulfill our role. We can call it the *book of role descriptions,* written by Society. Each and every person living in a particular society is downloaded with this *book of role descriptions*.

Everyone knows the description of his/her role and also knows the description of the role of others. For example, this book tells you *how a wife should and shouldn't behave, how a husband should and shouldn't behave, how a parent should and behave, how a friend should and shouldn't behave, how a child should behave and shouldn't, how a teacher should and shouldn't behave, how a doctor should and shouldn't behave, etc.* Automatically it gives rise to certain expectations.

155

You expect others to play their part right, by the book. They expect you to play your role right. In other words, everyone is judging everyone else. This is the basis of *Judging*. All morality is derived from this book of role descriptions. If there were no book of role descriptions, there would be no judging; there would be no morality.

Now what happens if someone doesn't play his or her part right? You get frustrated and at times, angry. It's actually your Acquired Self who feels let down, frustrated and angry, because it is the Acquired Self who builds up expectations. Your Acquired Self believes in all of the ideas contained in the book of role descriptions.

The closer the relationship is, the higher the expectations...and more emotional pain if someone does not meet your expectations. This emotional pain manifests as annoyances, frustrations and anger.

True Freedom from Expectations

To be free of annoyance and anger, you need to be free of expectations. You may hear someone advise, "you shouldn't have any expectations." But why not, you ask? Aren't expectations a part of normal daily living? How can you even function if there are no expectations?

It is true that most of the world revolves around expectations. Why? Because most of the world is in the grip of the Acquired Self, the conditioned mind. That is one major reason why most people feel frustrated, annoyed and angry. Only if people knew that their REAL Self, the one they are born with, had no expectations whatsoever! It's the Acquired Self who builds up all of the expectations and gets hurt when these expectations are not met.

With this realization, you can be free of expectations. Once you get rid of the root cause, then frustration, annoyance and anger simply do not arise. Then you don't have to practice certain techniques to be free of anger.

156

2. Self-righteousness

Another common reason for anger and frustration is self-righteousness.

What is self-righteousness? In simple terms, it means, "I am right." It also implies that "you are wrong." This is the root cause of all disagreements, disputes, arguments, quarrels, fights, lawsuits, battles and wars, all of which obviously create a huge amount of anger.

With few exceptions, everyone suffers from self-righteousness. Interestingly, people don't like to be called self-righteous because it's considered a bad quality. They don't think they are self-righteous, but they readily see it among others. They simply judge others to be self-righteous and don't go any deeper. Actually, they believe they are *right* that someone else is self-righteous. Interesting, isn't it?

Self-righteousness is an extremely common affliction and one of the reasons for all human conflicts. If we want to understand human conflicts, it makes sense to look at self-righteousness more deeply.

What is the Basis of Self-Righteousness?

Why do we believe that we are right and others are wrong? For example, for the same event, different people will have different opinions. Each one believes that he is right and others are wrong. The event is the same, but its interpretations are very different. Obviously, the problem lies in the interpretations. Now who is it that is doing the interpretation? It's your Acquired Self, isn't it? What is the Acquired Self? It's knowledge, concepts, ideas and stories about your own experiences, others experiences and collective human experiences, etc. Basically it consists of tons and tons of information and associated emotions residing inside you which you acquire as you grow up.

157

Typically when a person looks at an event, he interprets that event against the background of the already stored information and emotions in his Acquired Self. Obviously this stored information and emotions varies from person to person. Therefore, interpretation of the same event varies from person to person. With few exceptions, it is the Acquired Self who interprets events. Most people are in the grip of their Acquired Selves. They completely identify with their Acquired Self. That's who they believe they are! Therefore, they strongly believe that their interpretation of the event is *right.*

If we look deeper at the composition of a person's Acquired Self, we find that the *book of role descriptions* is an important part of it. This book, as we observed earlier, describes how a person *should* and *should not* behave in a given society. In addition to creating expectations, it also provides a background against which everyone keeps judging others behavior. It tells you and everyone else "what is *right* and what is *wrong*"; "what is *virtue* and what is *evil.*" This is the basis of *morality.*

These are basically concepts given to you by your Society. Using these concepts, everyone judges others and society judges everyone living in it. Now if you are in the total grip of your Acquired Self, you believe these concepts to be the *truth.* You honestly believe that you are *right* because you believe in certain concepts and those who don't believe in those concepts are *wrong.* Which of course is *self-righteousness.*

In the grip of self-righteousness, you are constantly annoyed and at times angry with those who do not believe in the same concepts as you do. Your Acquired Self believes that you are right and others are wrong.

In addition to the *book of role descriptions*, your Society also downloads into your Acquired Self, many other concepts. For example, it gives you the concepts about "your rights," "human rights" and "animal rights." All of these concepts become part of your Acquired Self and give you more ammunition to be *right*. These concepts strengthen your self-righteousness.

When you are in the grip of your Acquired Self, theses concepts become your *beliefs*. When others don't follow what you believe in, you get frustrated and angry.

In addition, your Society downloads into your Acquired Self the knowledge of history, which primarily is an interpretation of certain events by the Acquired Self of the historian-writer. That is the reason why there are so many different interpretations of the same events and of course, every historian believes he is right. The historian's interpretation of events becomes part of your Acquired Self and you believe them to be absolutely true (although the event may have happened before you and the historian were even born). Different Acquired Selves with different versions of the same historic event or historic figure then get into heated arguments and get angry at each other.

With this background, your Acquired Self also judges current political events. Usually, it is some so called expert who does it for you, on a TV show, in a newspaper or in a book. Acquired Selves with different versions of history interpret current events differently and each one believes he is right. With this background, people get into heated arguments and get mad and angry at each other.

It is interesting to note that in a given society there are collective concepts about what is right and what is wrong. This creates a *collective self-righteousness*, which gets reinforced constantly by the news media in that society. *What is right in one society may be wrong in another society.* This creates conflict between various societies. That's why people living in one society get angry at another society. This is the basis of *collective conflict, anger and violence* between various nations.

Then, within a given society, there are various concepts about what is right and what is wrong, depending upon various social, political and religious groups in that society. This creates conflict, anger and violence between various groups within a society.

Then within a group, there are various concepts about what is right and what is wrong. Therefore, within the same group, people get angry and fight amongst each other. Even within a family, there are various concepts about what is right and what is wrong. It leads to conflict, anger and violence (usually verbal but sometimes even physical) between various members of the same family. For example, you may be a strong believer in one political party and your wife may not agree with you. This could lead to a serious argument and verbal conflict.

Then, within an individual, there are conflicting concepts what is right and what is wrong. There is one code of ethics for the work place and another one for home, one code of ethics for friends and another one for enemies, one standard for yourself and another one for everyone else.

It all boils down to the virtual "I". Based on the concepts attached to "I", you judge everyone else out there as either your friend or enemy. That's how you perceive other people - as either your friends or your enemies: at home, in your neighborhood, at your work place, in your social, political or religious group, in your country and in the world. You stay annoyed and angry with your enemies, which often leads to violence, verbal as well as physical.

<u>True Freedom from Self-Righteousness.</u>

Once you have logical insight into the mechanics of self-righteousness, you will happily get out of the prison of self-righteousness. With that, anger automatically dies out.

3. Fear

Another reason why people get angry is their deep-seated *fear*, but they usually don't know it. Usually the more short-tempered a person is on the surface, the more fearful he

160

is inside. Expressing anger outwardly is a gesture of extreme insecurity inside. People try to scare others with their anger while they are fearful themselves. How ironic!

Most people don't even realize that their "bursts of anger" are actually arising out of a volcano of fear and insecurity.

If you are serious about getting to the bottom of the root causes of your anger, you have to examine yourself sincerely. Quite likely you will find that you feel quite fearful and insecure inside.

The Root Cause of Fear

Fear actually arises from the memory of a bad event, which has become part of your Acquired Self. Your Acquired Self learns from this bad event and says, "this should never happen to me again". However, then comes another thought - "what if" and that creates a huge amount of fear. In this way, your Acquired Self becomes quite insecure. Hence, it seeks security. In the pursuit of security, it wants to control the behavior of others. However, when it can't control others, it gets very angry. Even a trigger in the form of a news article or a story that reminds the Acquired Self that it cannot control others, can throw it into a rage.

True Freedom from Fear

People often try to *conquer* their fear by one technique or another. It may work temporarily but sooner or later, they are back in the grip of their fear.

Only when you know the root cause of fear, you can be free of it once for all. Then there is no need to learn various techniques to control your fear.

As we observed, fear arises from some bad memory in the past and the mind generating more thoughts in its effort to learn from it and prevent similar bad things from happening again. Once you realize that a "bad event" is not happening at this moment any longer. It happened, yes, but is not happening at this moment. It is being kept alive only through the activity of your mind. Otherwise, in reality, it is dead and gone. This realization will free you completely from fear.

Because the memory of a bad event does not control your mind anymore, there is no need to think this may happen again. Obviously, then your mind does not create more thoughts on how to prevent it. That's how the whole infrastructure of anger simply crumbles and you get the ultimate freedom from fear.

4. Insults

Another reason why people get angry is *insults*. Obviously you get angry when someone insults you. You *may or may not* express your anger.

Many people fight back by returning insulting remarks or gestures. Also, there are those who pretend to be polite and civilized on the surface while fuming with anger underneath. Later, they often express their anger while talking to their spouse or friends. Some even suppress anger so deeply that on the surface, they manage to remain polite and civilized all the time. They may even try to fake a smile, but deep inside, they feel irritated and don't even know why they feel that way!

What is the Basis of Insults?

In order to be truly free of insults, you first need to figure out, "who is it inside you who gets insulted in the first place."

Use logic and you will find that it's your Acquired Self who gets insulted. Your REAL Self, the one you are born with, never used to get insulted. Why do I say that? This is because a newborn baby never gets insulted. You can try to insult a baby by saying whatever you want, but the baby will not be insulted. In the same way, imagine someone trying to insult you in a language or through gestures that you don't understand.

Obviously, you will not be insulted. Therefore, we can conclude that for the insult to occur, one has to understand the *concepts* attached to those words and gestures. Otherwise, they have no power.

Where do you learn the words and gestures and all of the concepts attached to them? You are *not* born with them. You obviously learn them as you grow up in a certain society.

With every word, there is a concept attached. For example, the word STUPID has a whole concept of unintelligence, inadequacy and worthlessness attached to it. When your developing Acquired Self learns this word, it stores all the negative concepts attached to the word. When someone calls you by that word, the negative concept attached to that word is activated and negative thoughts trigger negative emotions. You feel unintelligent, worthless, inadequate and angry. *You didn't deserve it. How dare someone say that.* Actually, your Acquired Self's sense of self-esteem is threatened. Therefore, it fights back verbally or even physically in order to secure its existence, its self-esteem.

Society's Collective Acquired Self downloads the concept of *"insult and respect"* into your Acquired Self. When others respect you, your Acquired Self feels validated and when others insult you, your Acquired Self feels humiliated. In other words, your Acquired Self is constantly reacting to how others treat it. Your Acquired Self wants to be respected and not be insulted. Obviously, it has no control over others' behavior, but it doesn't know this basic fact. It just keep searching for respect and running away from insult. It is especially true if at an early age you were insulted (teased) a lot. Your Acquired Self felt humiliated and all of those painful experiences become part of your Acquired Self. Then, your Acquired Self found a way (academics, sports, arts, etc.) for others to start respecting you. Your Acquired Self finally got the praise and validation it was so hungry for. Naturally, your Acquired Self works hard on this track and usually ends up being quite accomplished and successful in that field. With each step of success, it gets more respect, praise and validation and it loves it all. *The more it gets attached to respect, the more it resents the idea of insult.* Then a trivial teasing remark can upset your Acquired Self for days. You may even burst into anger in social situation where you didn't get enough respect, which you perceive as an insult.

True Freedom from Insults

Often others (usually those who care about you) can see your overreactions and suggest anger management. So you try the usual venues society offers such as counseling, books, seminars, etc. But nothing really works for you. Sooner or later, you again explode in a rage or you sizzle inside over some insulting remark someone made days ago. Often, you get even more annoyed, even ashamed, that you are holding grudges because you know that's a bad thing. Most people stay trapped in the prison of insults for the rest of their life.

Is it possible to be free of insults? The answer is yes, but only when you get to the root of the problem. When you realize that it is your Acquired Self that gets insulted, you can be free of insults by freeing your self from your Acquired Self. Then you realize that it is your Acquired Self who is holding onto painful memories when it felt insulted. Those painful experiences are not happening in the present moment, but only happening in your head. This simple realization can free you of the huge load of painful memories. You also realize that you don't have to keep proving your worth and being praised by others. The need for praise simply vanishes. Then, you don't react to remarks of praise or insult. People can say whatever they want: it does not make you elated or angry.

Free of your Acquired Self, you live in joy and peace that is never threatened.

Once you fully realize the mechanics of insulting words, you'll laugh (in your head) when someone uses an insulting remark, won't you? Because you will see that the other person's Acquired Self is doing what it has been conditioned to do and in reality, it does not mean a thing. Then there is no need to fight back.

It is quite likely that even with all this wisdom, your Acquired Self may engage and fight back next time you're insulted. However, minutes or even hours later, you will be able to see the "real mechanics of insult."

The moment you see insult in its true colors, you'll be free of it, instead of fuming for days. Next time, in the middle of an insult, you may see your own Acquired Self getting engaged and trying to fight back. Simply seeing your monster in action will free you of its tight hold on you. You may actually burst into laughter. In this way, no one will be able to insult you. *People may try to insult you, but you won't get insulted.*

Q: I worry a lot. I have tried various techniques but nothing seems to work. I know I am not supposed to worry. It is not good for me. Any help!

A: It is true that worrying is not good for anyone. And many people know this basic fact, but they still continue to worry. They know that most things they worry about never happen but they still continue to worry. They try different techniques, which often don't work. Then they feel frustrated, as they are unable to control their worrying mind. They may feel like losers in addition to being worried. Many end up on sedatives, anti-anxiety or anti-depression medications. The drugs may temporarily lessen the emotions attached with anxiety but worrying still continues. People feel *imprisoned* by a worrying mind. They don't see any way out and may actually get depressed.

Is it possible to be free of the worrying mind? If you are earnest to find the answer, you, first need to dig deep and find out, "Why do you worry?" If you observe you will find out that you worry about various bad things that may happen in the future. Your mind is busy, thinking, "what if," "what may," what will I ————. And it tries to prepare itself to deal with these hypothetical situations. It creates whole mental pictures of hypothetical bad situations and then tries to find a solution. Because the situations are hypothetical, therefore the solutions are also hypothetical and don't quite seem to satisfy you. So you try to find more answers. The search for more answers add in more variables into the possibilities of "what if" and your mind remains preoccupied with the endless movie of "What if."

Therefore the culprit of worrying is your busy mind, isn't it? Next question you have to ask is, why does your mind think in this way?

If you use logic, you will find out that's how your mind is conditioned, isn't it. Right from your childhood, your mind gets conditioned by your society to create hypothetical dangerous situations and create hypothetical solutions, isn't it? Fire drills,

166

earthquake drills, terrorist-attack drills are some of the examples.

Society also downloads into your mind all sorts of information about possible dangerous situations and how to cope with them. "Bird flue, Swine flue, cancer, heart attack are some of the examples. Society is continuously preparing your mind about all of the possible dangers out there.
Then your conditioned mind does exactly what it is conditioned to do: trying to figure out all of the possible dangers and how to prevent or cope with them. In doing so, it creates a huge amount of worries for you.

Now you understand, the root cause of your worries is your conditioned mind. And your conditioned mind is what you think you are. That's why you believe in all of the information that has been downloaded into your conditioned mind by your society. This is your Acquired Self.

As long as you are identified with your Acquired Self, you will continue to believe in what it thinks and you will continue to worry.

Only when you realize that you are not your Acquired Self, you are free of it. With this realization, you automatically get freedom from all the conditioned thought patterns in your conditioned mind. Then you don't believe in what your thoughts imply. Then you treat your thoughts as simple thoughts, no more. You fully realize whatever your thoughts *imply* is not real. Why? Because whatever your thought imply, is never happening in front of your eyes. Then you don't worry about what your thoughts say. This is because you realize them to be mere thoughts, no more. Whatever they say is NOT REAL. With this realization, you get freedom from your busy worrying mind without using any techniques.

167

Q: My husband does not listen to me. I know I am right. But each time I try to tell him what he should not be doing, he becomes defensive and we get into a fight. It makes me so frustrated and upset. I am trying to communicate as everyone says but it is not working. I can't live like this. What else can I do!!

A: What you are doing is obviously not working. Therefore, you have to find another way. It is encouraging that you have realized that you can't live like this, and you are willing to try another way.

Have you ever wondered who you really are? Use logic and you will realize that you were you before you got married and became a wife. You were you before you went to school. And you were you before you started to talk or walk or crawl. *Indeed you were you when you were born.* Right!

Now take a deep breath and don't think anymore for a minute. Shift your attention into the Now: What you see, hear, smell, taste and touch. Also become aware of the space, silence and stillness. Take attention into your chest and feel an inner peace. Don't believe what I say. Simply experience the REALITY - the GOD inside you, as you did when you were a newborn baby.

As you grew up, your mind got conditioned. It acquired all kind of ideas and concepts. Then your REAL Self got stuck to this Acquired Self.

As a grown up, you, like the vast majority of humans, identify with the Acquired Self and think that's who you are. Being *wife* is part of your Acquired Self; it is a concept you acquired from your society. But you don't even realize that it is a concept. You start believing in it as if this was some kind of truth. You were you before you became a wife, isn't it!

In the same way you (and almost every one else on the planet) have acquired a lot of ideas and concepts and don't even see them as concepts. *Then you look at life thru these*

168

concepts. You *judge, interpret* and *expect* according to these concepts. That's why you feel so strongly that you are *right* and your husband is *wrong*. Guess what, your husband believes that he is right and you are wrong. That thinking obviously creates conflict between the two of you. Each one of you talk to each other and let the other person know your position and expect the other person to listen to you, which really means, that the other person should change according to your wishes. *You both try to change each other.* It is like a war and each one of you wants to prevail. No one wants to be defeated. You and society calls it *communication?*

Who is at war? It is your Acquired Self against your husband's Acquired Self. As long as you stay in the grip of your Acquired self, you will continue to try to win the war, because Acquired Self hates to lose. You will continue to try to change your husband, and he will continue to try to change you. No one will surrender and the war will continue, causing huge amount of suffering for yourself and your husband.

It's only when you realize that it's your Acquired Self who is at war that you can rise above it and be free of it. Then you realize that there is no need to win, no need to control others' behavior, no need to be worried about future or stay furious over the past because both are virtual and don't exist, except in your head. You automatically stop worrying about future and completely let go of the past; you stop criticizing and judging your husband.

This internal change inside you brings you true inner peace that shines through - The peace of GOD. Your husband senses this change in you and starts to change himself even though you have no wishes or expectations for him to change. That's how marital conflicts end for good.

Beware of your Acquired Self. It will put down all kinds of roadblocks such as: *"It does not make any sense" "Why should I change; I know I am right and he is wrong, therefore he is the one who should change."* In this way Acquired Self would love to keep you in a deadlock. But treat these thoughts as thoughts and no more. Thoughts that want to keep you trapped in misery. Once you don't let thoughts dictate your behavior, you are free of them and you are free of your Acquired Self. Then you will see your husband as another human being imprisoned by his own Acquired self. Instead of being angry, you will have compassion for him. All of the changes will happen in you and these changes radiate and will likely influence your husband as well.

Be careful *not* to start trying to *enlighten* your husband. Although it is quite tempting! If he is not ready, he will resist and before you know it, you will be in the grip of your own Acquired Self, and the whole emotional drama will start to replay.
Your job is to be free of your own Acquired Self and that's all.

When you live in the Now, you get in touch with an everlasting inner peace and joy. There is no anger, jealousy, guilt or bitterness. There is No fear or anxiety about the future because you realize that the future does not exist except in your thoughts. You realize that *Now* is real and past and future are virtual. In the *Now*, there is no stress, whatsoever.

Once you are grounded in the Now, you can *utilize* your Acquired Self to live in society. Then you clearly see that as a wife you are simply fulfilling a role and no more. You play this role as best as you can. You understand the demands this role brings upon you. But you never get taken over by it, or you never get consumed by it. With this realization all the heaviness associated with being a wife simply goes away.

Q: I am a happy upbeat person but I go through periods when I feel 'low" and it takes a while to get out of these lows. Basically, I get annoyed and upset at the comments people make. Sometimes they are so rude and insensitive. I especially get hurt at the insulting rude comments my husband makes. I try to ignore, try to let go, but it really does not work. What should I do?

A: First of all, let me tell you the simple truth that you probably wouldn't like. The real problem is not your husband or other rude, insensitive people. *The real problem resides inside you.* The good news is that because the problem resides inside you, you can take care of it, without changing anyone else. It's all in your hands! You don't have to depend on anyone else to change his or her behavior at all.

Why do you get hurt when people make rude and insensitive comments? Because you don't expect them to do so, especially someone close to you, your husband, your friend, your mother etc. You *expect* people to be nice and sensitive, especially your husband, but they let you down.

You feel happy, upbeat, when other people are nice and polite to you. So, it is logical to conclude that you react to other peoples' comments and become sad or happy.

Let me ask you a question. "Do you know who you really are?" If I may point out, *you are not who you think you are.*

Let me explain why I say this. Obviously you think you are a wife, a professional, a friend, a nice person, and a polite, sensitive person ------.

Use logic, and you will realize that all of these are actually concepts. And what you think you are, is actually a bundle of concepts, isn't it. A phantom, an illusion.

You were *not* born with these concepts. These were downloaded into you by the society in which you grew up. We can call it "your Acquired Self."

Every society downloads into the Acquired Self of its citizens all sorts of concepts. One group of such concepts revolves around how everyone in the society *should and shouldn't behave*. For example, everyone should be nice and polite to others, and should not be rude or insensitive to others.

Everyone learns this 'book of role descriptions" and this book becomes part of the Acquired Self of every person in that society. Then, everyone *expects*, as well as *judges* others according to this book.

When others are polite to you, your Acquired Self *judges* them to be good people which makes you happy. When you are polite to others, it makes you happy, as you are playing according to the book, which makes you a good person.

But, when others are *rude* to you, your Acquired Self *judges* them to be bad people which makes you sad and mad, especially when it is someone close to you. This is because you have higher expectations from those who are close to you.

You will continue to be on the rollercoaster of happiness and sadness and madness, as long as you are identified with your Acquired Self.

Use logic, and you will realize that in order to be free of happiness, sadness and madness, you ought to be free of your expectations. In order to be free of expectations, you ought to be free of your Acquired Self.

How do you get freedom from your Acquired Self? Just having the insight that it is *not* truly who you are. You were not born with this. You acquired it as result of conditioning from the society as you grew up. You may want to sit down and write down all the concepts that society gave you as it conditioned your mind. A list of all what are actually concepts and not real you, such as concepts of wife, husband, friend, nice person, polite person, sensitive person, good person, bad person etc.

Once you realize the conceptual, virtual nature of "Me" residing inside you, you are mentally free of it. And it is a true liberation, true freedom!

Once you are free of your Acquired Self, you realize that everyone else in society is in the *prison* of their Acquired Self, and is suffering from a psychological ailment, as you were. When their Acquired Self makes an insulting or insensitive comment, you realize it is their Acquired Self making this comment. Obviously, you don't get upset because you have no expectations, as you are free of your Acquired Self. In addition, when their Acquired Selves make some compliment, you realize it is their Acquired Self making this comment. Obviously, you don't get elated.

With this wisdom, you are completely free of the rollercoaster of happiness, sadness and madness.

After you are free from your Acquired Self, you then realize the relative, secondary significance Acquired Self has. Then, you utilize it to function in the society. You utilize it when it is necessary, and shut it off as soon as it is not needed. Then you continue to play the role of a wife but you are not seriously caught up in the expectations.

Once, you are free of your Acquired Self, you treat every other person, including your husband as a human being, because you realize that's who really every person is: a human being, no more, no less. Then you disregard any *nasty* or *flattering* comments from any one as a silly, childish play of their Acquired Self, no more!

As a practical guide, just remember: Keep your mind where your body is. See what you see, hear what you hear, smell what you smell, feel what you touch and taste what you taste. In addition, take attention inside your body, especially your chest. You will feel an immense energy flowing throughout

173

your body. This is the *joy* that is always there, in the absence of any flattering comments.

Q: I have so many responsibilities. I have no time for myself.

Many people feel that they don't have time for themselves because they have so many responsibilities. They feel rushed all the time, which creates a feeling of pressure, nervousness and restlessness. They are also afraid that they may *not* be able to fulfill their responsibilities, say as a mother, as a father or as a daughter. They are afraid that they may fail themselves or other loved ones. They also resent that they don't have time for themselves. In other words they develop emotional burden of nervousness, fear, and resentment. In more severe cases, it leads to anxiety, anger and depression.

Now lets take a deeper look what's happening under the surface. It is obvious that "responsibilities" are the root of the problem. What is the origin of responsibilities?
Was there ever a time when you did not have responsibilities? I mean, absolutely free of any responsibilities. Using logic, it is obvious that you were not born with all of these responsibilities. Right!

At birth, no one has any responsibilities. The original REAL Self is devoid of responsibilities. Then, as we grow up, we are told by our parents, teachers, books, movies, magazines and society, in general, what our responsibilities are as a child, as a student, as a worker, as a citizen, as a spouse, as a parent etc. Therefore, all responsibilities are part of the Acquired Self. We acquire them but we are not born with them.

Now let us see what a responsibility is?
A responsibility is that you are expected to do certain things. Every society has created a "book of role descriptions" for various roles that a person plays, and everyone learns this book.

For example, as a parent, as a spouse, as a child, as a student, as a worker, as a boss, you know what you are expected to do and you also know what others are expected to do. Everyone is supposed to follow this book. Now if for one

175

reason or another, you can't do your role according to the book, who gets disappointed? It's you, isn't it? This is the basis of self-criticism and guilt. And if others don't follow the book, who gets upset and disappointed? It's you, isn't it!

Right from your childhood, your Acquired Self also learns that there are bad consequences if you don't do what you are supposed to do. You may be punished physically or verbally. *Some of the examples of verbal punishment: you are a failure; you just cannot do it right, do you? You are a disappointment for the family or for the school or for the company.*

Therefore, you develop this *compulsion* to fulfill your responsibilities or you will be punished. Mostly, you punish yourself; your inner voice, your monster within, your Acquired Self keeps reminding you that you do not want to be a *failure.* This inner voice also says, remember *losers* are made fun of, they don't get anywhere in life, they are punished and don't get rewarded. In some cases, this inner voices may even say that you will be punished in the *life after death,* if you did not carry out your responsibilities.

Perhaps, now you understand why you have such a compulsion to carry out your responsibilities, and why you live under constant fear of failing yourself or others.

Where does this feeling of not "having any time for myself"come from. If you look at it closely and with honesty, you will find that it is an activity of the "I", the core of the Acquired Self. Under the surface, you will find yourself saying, "I do all these activities for others as a duty, I have no other choice and I end up wasting all my precious time, and no time is left for myself." Of course, this creates *resentment* and in more severe cases *anger* and *depression.*

So what's the solution?

Just an insight that all responsibilities are given to you by your society, and you were not born with these, is a major breakthrough for most people. With this realization, you are no longer in the grip of your Acquired Self. Consequently, the emotional *compulsion* to do every little responsibility goes away.

It does not mean that you stop carrying out your responsibilities. Not at all. Now you carry out your responsibilities with a different *attitude*. You understand that to live in society, you fulfill various roles according to the "book of role descriptions" written by society. These roles are just the roles that you play. But roles are not you. In REAL, *You are your REAL Self devoid of any responsibilities*. This realization has tremendous potential for your transformation.

Then, you play your roles as best as you can. You also realize that the concepts of success, failure, reward and punishment are also part of the Acquired Self. So, you are *not* afraid of failing as a parent, child, teacher, doctor etc. Neither, do you feel guilty if you tried, but could *not* fulfill your role according to the book.

Then, you carry your roles without the heavy emotional burden of *compulsion, fear, nervousness, anxiety* and *guilt*. The heaviness of life gets lifted off you. You have freed your self from the grip of the Acquired Self. Then, you do these activities with full *attention* and enjoy them fully. For example, you are carrying your kids to soccer game, and you are enjoying it. If you are cooking for the family, you are in the moment and enjoying it. There is no need for "my time" because such thinking is part of the Acquired Self. *In fact, all the time is your time if you stay in the present moment.* You will be free of any resentment that may arise out of carrying out your responsibilities. Because, you realize these are not responsibilities or duties imposed on you. Rather, you have elected these roles and you carry out these roles with joy as apart of living in the society harmoniously. Can you taste the transformation?

177

Q: I feel tired. Doctors say I don't a medical reason to be tired. Could it be stress although I don't seem to have any thing to stress about.

A: One of the main reasons people feel tired is stress. There are medical conditions that can cause tiredness. But once you have been given a clean bill of health by your doctor, the main reason for your tiredness may be your stress.

Lets examine how stress causes tiredness. Stress is of two types, inner stress and outer stress. Most people have inner stress most of the time, although on the surface, life seems good, as there are no stressful situations.

Inner stress, on the other hand is caused by your busy mind, even though, on the surface you don't have any stress. Have you ever observed that your busy mind never rests? Like a radio, it continues to talk in your head. Even when you are relaxing in a chair, at home and no work needs to be done, you busy mind is talking. It simply never stops. Even during sleep, it is busy most of the time, creating dreams.

Most of the time, your busy mind is talking about the *past* or the *future*. The *monologue* goes like this:

Why did it happen...........
it should not have happened............
It should have happened.............
what if............
what may............
what will I do if..............................

Mind is either dissatisfied with the past and tries to change it, or it is preparing itself to deal with a virtual fearful situation in the future. To the body, pictures painted by these thoughts are real, as if these events are happening right now, although both past and future are not real at this moment. *Past is dead and gone and future never arrives.* But body cannot distinguish between what is happening right now in real and what is not, which, in fact, is the function of the mind. And when

178

the source, the mind is dysfunctional, creating stories of the past and case scenarios of the future, body reacts to these stories and case scenarios as if these are real and happening right now. *In this way, body lives in a continuous low-grade fear, dissatisfaction, and unhappiness.* Perhaps now you understand why such a body will feel *tired*.

And there is a physiological basis of this tiredness. As a result of these negative emotions, body releases various chemicals such as cortisol and adrenaline into the blood stream. Excess amounts of cortisol and adrenaline wreck havoc on various organs and systems in your body. That's how a busy mind causes tiredness, and also contributes to a host of medical and psychological illnesses.

So What's the Solution?

Can you observe your busy mind? See for yourself how it keeps you imprisoned in the past or in the future. By using logic can you tell your self that the past is dead, not real anymore and future is simply an illusion. Past and future are both virtual and exist only in your mind, isn't it? With this insight, you get out of the prison of the past and the future, whenever you find yourself in it. *Instantaneously you free yourself from dissatisfactions, resentments, frustrations and worries.*

Pay attention to your reality: the present moment created by your five senses i.e. sight, hearing, taste, smell and touch. There is no inner stress when you start living in this manner. There may be outer stressful situations. You deal with them as they arise. But you no longer create them in your head.

Whenever you are by yourself at home, close your eyes and pay attention to your breathing. Thoughts will come, try to distract you but you simply observe them, and you also fully realize that they are simply thoughts; what they are pointing to is not real at this time. You keep your attention on your breathing; follow breath into your chest and follow it out of your nose. Observe how your chest rises and falls. Once your mind settles down you will experience immense sense of *aliveness* and *joy* inside your body. It is hard to explain but you can experience it. This aliveness is always inside you. Try to stay in this field of aliveness and joy as much as you can. Your tiredness will simply evaporate.

Q: I am becoming forgetful. What's happening to me? I am quite worried.

A: There are various medical conditions for forgetfulness. See a doctor and make sure you don't have any of these conditions.

Stress, however plays a significant role in causing forgetfulness and memory loss. As we observed earlier in the book, inner stress comes from a busy mind, which most people are afflicted with. A busy mind is a scattered mind, running in ten different directions, which over a period of time, can lead to *forgetfulness*. Another way to think of this is that mind eventually gets exhausted from staying busy all the time without any rest.

So, What's the Solution?

Can you be aware of your busy mind? How it loves to stay in the past and in the future? How it generates negative thoughts and associated negative emotions?

Bring awareness to whatever you do. *Keep your mind where your body is*. For example, if you are driving, keep your mind on the road. At work pay full attention what are you doing. When you are putting your keys down, pay attention where you are putting them.

And when you are resting, put your mind to rest as well. *You do this by observing your field of awareness created by your five senses but without any interpreting, judging or comparing.* For example, you are sitting in a room waiting for your doctor to arrive. Instead of make your mind even busier by submerging into a magazine, look around. See various objects in the room, and outside the window. Observe various sounds you hear. Feel the air. Sense the texture of the chair you are sitting in. You observe all this without interpreting, judging or comparing. Soon, you may find yourself *liking* or *disliking* the paintings or the furniture in the room. You may not like the color of the room or the style of the chairs. These are all activities of the Acquired Self your busy mind is active. *You need to simply be in the room, and observe things as they are.*

Whenever you have time for yourself, spend it in this manner. Don't keep it busy by turning to the TV or Internet or newspapers and magazines. Also keep your conversations to whatever is necessary. Avoid unnecessary chitchatting, as you are wasting your brain energy. Just be aware whatever you do. *Then you mind will start getting some rest. A rested mind works a whole lot better than a tired busy mind.*

When you pay full attention to whatever you are doing, you become *aware* of what you are doing. Then, you become more proficient whatever you do. When you live in this manner, you have no stress, and your forgetfulness simply disappears.

Q: I want peace in this world full of violence. What can I do?

A: For a moment, take a deep breath, relax, and shift your attention in the Now.

Then use simple logic. First of all, take a look at your question, and figure out who is this "I" who "wants" peace in the world full of violence. Isn't this your conditioned mind, your Acquired Self who is pretending to be you? This "You" is looking thru the filters of concepts in your head: the concepts of war and peace, violence and nonviolence, vice and virtue, the bad and good, etc.

Use simple logic, and you will find out these concepts have been in existence as long as human civilization has. Then, ask yourself a question. Have these concepts been able to establish peace on the planet? The answer is pretty obvious.

Now if you are sincere in eradicating violence from the world, first you will have to find out, "why is there violence in the world," in the first place. In order to cure it, you have to accurately diagnose it, at its root cause. Right! On the other hand, if you keep patching it without treating the root cause of any illness, you will not be able to treat that disease. For example, you keep giving Tylenol to treat fever due to pneumonia eventually the patient may die of infection while having no fever.

Therefore, isn't it necessary to look deeply into "why is there violence in the world," if you truly want to do something about. Use simple logic, and you will find out that violence happens when there is *conflict*. Two people or two nations have a conflict. Then they fight, verbally or physically. Right!

Interestingly, each of the two people (or nations) feels that he is right and the other one is wrong. What makes a person think that he is right and other person is wrong? This is obviously, the concept of "what is right" and "what is wrong". But, that person does not think of it as a concept. He believes in it as if it was the truth. Why? Because concepts are the backbone of the Acquired Self, and Acquired Self obviously has to believe in those concepts to be the truth for it to survive. Seeing those concepts, as concepts will be suicide for the Acquired Self.

In the grip of the Acquired Self, everyone believes that he is right and those who don't agree with him are wrong. In this way, *concepts divide human beings from each other, and that is the basis of conflict, and violence.*

Violence can be verbal or physical. You see violence everywhere: individuals arguing, yelling, and fighting with each other all the time everywhere, with everyone believing that he is right and the other person is wrong. Collectively, groups of people believing in one concept, fight with another group of people who are against that concept. This is the basis of "One political party fighting with another, one social group fighting with another, and one religious institution fighting with another religious institution. This is the basis of battles and wars between various tribes and nations.

It is pretty clear that concepts are the basis of human conflict and violence. Obviously, another concept, however *noble* it may be, is not going to get rid of the root cause of violence in the world. That's why there is so much violence in the world despite so many wonderful, noble ideas promoting peace and nonviolence.

Therefore, isn't it necessary that you get rid of concepts inside you; be free of your Acquired Self. Freedom from concepts automatically restores peace in you. World is nothing but an outward expression of you and you are an inward reflection of the world outside. You bring peace in the outside world by bringing peace to the world inside you. That's all!

Q: I feel great when I am giving advice to others. But, I still feel annoyed and irritated inside. I should be very happy. I don't understand why?

A: Everyone loves to give advice to others. But, who is really giving advice? Look carefully and you will realize that it's your Acquired Self that loves to give advice to others.

Giving advice also makes your Acquired Self feel better, superior and worthwhile. It boosts up your ego. That's why you love to give advice, even if you may not have been asked for it. Often, your advice is *tainted* by your own selfish motives, although you may not be aware of it.

Next time observe your conversation. You will be surprised how often you are giving advice. Once you give advice, you also create expectations (you expect your friends or the loved ones to follow your advice) and if they don't follow your advice, you get disappointed, hurt and irritated.

Q: What should I do when someone asks for advice?

A: Don't reply immediately. Listen carefully; be aware of your own Acquired Self, who is always ready to give advice as a *knee jerk reflex*. If possible, ask for some time to think it over. Then, once you are alone, get still by watching your breathing and being in the field of awareness.

Once your own mental noise has calmed down, simply ask the question, and stay in your field of awareness. Sooner or later, the answer will pop up. This answer will be the answer without the fingerprints of your own Acquired Self and may truly help your friend or ~~the~~ loved ones.

Q: I get so stressed out arranging "fundraisers" for a noble cause. But I cannot say no, otherwise I feel guilty. What should I do?

A: We live in a conceptual, virtual world, in which there are all sorts of concepts including *noble* concepts.

The virtual human world is created by the collective human mind. Then, each individual mind is downloaded with concepts from this collective human world. In this way, there is a "baby" in your head, your Acquired Self, which is produced by the Collective virtual human world, the "Papa." The two interact with each other, and feed off each other.

Your Acquired Self has acquired a noble concept to donate your time for some noble cause. Often, it involves raising money, which involves arranging fundraisers, which is quite demanding, and create a lot of stress for you. Even though, you get stressed out arranging these fundraisers, it is your Acquired Self that cannot say "No." "How could you not support a noble cause?" An inner voice generated by your Acquired Self surfaces, and triggers the emotion of guilt.

Can you see how your Acquired Self is in the driver's seat, in total control of your thoughts, emotions and actions? Any concept, even noble concept is part of your Acquired Self, and it keeps you trapped in the collective conceptual world. In fact, all the time you devote to a noble cause, you are away from the Reality of Now-the God. You may be working for a noble cause in the name of a conceptual god, which actually keeps you away from the Real God. How ironic!

It is interesting to observe that the human mind creates a concept of every reality it encounters. For example in the Real world, there are forms. But human mind has created the concepts of trees, animals, planets etc. It gives them names such as a pine tree, dog, Mars, etc . Then, It may even attach more labels such the same pine tree becomes a Christmas tree in the month of December. Then, it writes books about these concepts, create paintings, take pictures and make movies.

187

In the same way, human mind has also created the concept of god, based on the Reality of God. Then, people get stuck in the concept of god, which, in fact keeps them away from the REAL GOD - the Now - the Space, Silence and Stillness, in front of your eyes.

In this way, human mind has created a virtual, world, parallel to the Real world.

With this insight, you ~~are able to~~ rise above your Acquired self. Then you utilize it to function in the human world, but you don't take your Acquired and all of the concepts sitting in it, too seriously. You understand their conceptual, virtual nature. You spend *minimal* time in the conceptual world that is required to make a living for yourself and your family. As soon as you are done making a basic living for the day, you shift your attention into the Now. Experience what is Real, what you perceive with your five senses: what you see, hear, smell, taste and touch. When you see, also be aware of space that gives rise to all of the objects. Without space, there would be no objects. In the same way, when you hear, be aware of silence as well, which is always there. Sound comes out of silence and goes back into it. When see a movement, be aware of the stillness, which is always there, in the background of all movements. When you experience space, silence and stillness, you experience REAL God that no words can ever describe.

As far as the problems and the suffering in the human conceptual world are concerned, those are created by the collective human mind. See it for yourself. At the root of all human problems lie greed, hate, grievances, power struggles, self-righteousness, all of which are the products of concepts. The conceptual "I" surrounded by layers and layers of concepts, which constitutes your Acquired Self as well the collective conceptual human world. Stress, suffering and problems have always been, and will always be present in this conceptual human world. On the other hand, in the Real world, there is never any suffering, stress or problems.

Q: Why do people get so concerned that someone has to carry on the family name?

A: What is a family name? In Reality, it is a sound, but obviously, it has a concept attached to it. Therefore, it has huge significance in the Conceptual World. It gives your Acquired Self a sense of *belonging,* being *special,* which gives it a temporary sense of *security* that it is so *thirsty* for. Why? Because Acquired Self is Virtual: it does not exist in Real. Talk of the huge amount of insecurity it inhabits.

Your Acquired Self is *not* only immensely insecure, but it also seeks out immortality. It does not want to die, ever. One of the ways for it to perpetuate is through the family name. In this way, even if you are dead, your family name survives. Consequently, it can propagate through several generations. That's one of the reasons why certain cultures give so much importance to boys over girls. Boys can carry the family name, and girls usually can't.

In fact, your Acquired self does not die with your death. It gets perpetuated through your children. They often carry on your family name, traditions, culture, language, religion, and collective past in the form of genealogy. But this is all virtual!
In Real, it is space, stillness, silence, out there and inside you. REAL Self, which is simple awareness, consciousness. It is immortal. Even life is immortal. A life form comes to an end, but life continues.

It is clear that the conditioned human mind has created a virtual world of its own, which separates it from the Reality. Then it wants to live forever just like Reality. Consequently, it has invented several clever ways to perpetuate, like family name and it often successfully perpetuates. But irony is that it does *not* even exist. It is inherently virtual, non-existent.

Q: I am a very conscientious physician in the USA. Each time I hear someone got sued, I get very anxious and sometimes even have a panic attack. What can I do to prevent panic attacks?

A: See who is talking? Who is this "I". It is your Acquired Self, isn't it? Being a physician is part of your Acquired Self. That's who you think you are. The conceptual world makes it seem like a reality, but obviously it is not.

To the Acquired Self, the idea of losing a career is dreadful, especially if that person has put in a lot of time and effort into becoming a professional. Why? Because your career (a doctor, engineer or a CEO) becomes part of your identity, your Acquired Self. Even the *idea* of losing a part of it, your career, is obviously very threatening to your Acquired Self. *Your acquired self is afraid of its own death.*

Like everyone else, your Acquired Self harbors a lot of traumatic experiences (its own as well as those of others that it has heard about or read about) it calls "My past." And it keeps them alive at subconscious or even unconscious level. It knows that those experiences happened because it was not *in control*. Which creates a deep sense of *insecurity*. Naturally, your Acquired Self wants to be in control, in order to prevent these kinds of traumatic experiences from happening again. So it works hard, and achieves a certain *position* in the society. Now it feels in control, and has a *sense of security*. But the idea of losing its position (and its control) shakes up all of its security. Then it trembles inside, which leads to severe anxiety and panic attack.

Now what happens once you have the deep understanding that *you are not your Acquired Self*. This wisdom immediately frees your from all of the stress associated with your Acquired Self including all of the past, the insecurities and fears arising out of this past.

Then, you realize that being a physician (or any other professional) is a way to *make a living*, that's all. You no longer seek yourself thru your profession. You follow the rules that your society has created, including the rules that your medical board has created. You do the best you can to help your patients. But you also realize that all what you do is part of living in the conceptual world. In the real world, you were you before you became a doctor, and you will be you even if you lose your license to practice medicine due to a lawsuit. *You were true you the day you were born and you will still be you the day you die.* No lawsuit can ever take your true self REAL Self) away from you.

With this wisdom, your anxiety will subside. However, your Acquired Self has a lot of pull, and before you know it, you will be back in its grip.

Next time you have a panic attack, be still, *watch* your Acquired Self rising thru you like a monster and trying to take control of your thoughts to continue the vicious cycle of thoughts-fear-thoughts.

Feel the emotional havoc it creates for you, but don't get consumed by the emotion. *Be fully aware that you are not your Acquired Self. Shift your attention to the space, silence and stillness, around you and inside you.*

Not getting food from you in the form of your attention, your Acquired Self will soon start to subside. Remember each time your Acquired Self is unable to feed of you, it weakens. And each time it takes control of you, it gets stronger. Stay vigilant and eventually you will be totally free of anxiety and panic attacks.

Q: How do you deal with threats?

A: What is a threat? A danger to your survival. Threats are of two types:

Real threats:

In the real world, there can be a real threat in the form of a real danger. For example, you are in the wild and a lion jumps on you. Instantaneously your built in "Fight or Flight" response kicks in: your heart starts pumping blood at a much faster rate, your blood pressure goes up, your airways widen, your blood glucose goes up to provide extra fuel to your muscles, and your vision gets sharper. In this way, you are *primed* to either fight or run away. In either case there is no fear. If you survive, then thinking about "what might have happened" triggers a lot of fear.

Virtual threats:

Threats can be virtual. In fact, the conceptual virtual world is full of virtual threats. To the virtual conceptual world in your head (your Acquired Self), these threats seem real, especially because everyone else is in the same boat.

The problem arises when you *confuse* virtual threats with the real threats. Virtual threats are manufactured by the conditioned mind, individually as well as collectively. In fact, collective virtual threats are very powerful. Then, you act individually or collectively under the influence of these virtual threats. These actions often create more stress for you and the others.

Q: The threat of losing my job is real to me. How can I not worry about it? But I also know worrying is not good for me. What should I do?

A: Your job generates income, and is of course important to you. Use simple logic, and you realize your job is important because it supports your lifestyle, which is a product of your Acquired Self, who obviously perceives the thought of losing job as a threat to itself. "Without income how will I survive," a thought is generated by your conditioned mind, which is your Acquired Self. This thought of potential danger triggers the emotion of fear, which creates neurochemical changes in your brain. This altered neurochemical environment facilitates the production of more fearful thoughts which triggers more emotion of fear and a vicious cycle sets in. **Fear sucks up all of your attention. No room left for simple logic.** Then, you justify your fear by saying, "how can I not worry about my future." Since your childhood, your Acquired Self has been conditioned to *learn from the past and worry about the future*. You and everyone else in this world believe in this important concept.

As long as you are trapped in the virtual world in your head as your Acquired Self and the conceptual, virtual world, we call the world, you will continue to worry about future, no matter how many times you hear that worrying is not good for you.

So what is the Solution?

First of all, get out of the virtual world by using your five senses: see what you see, hear what you hear, smell what you smell, feel what you touch and taste what you taste. Also be aware of space, silence, and the stillness around you and inside you.

This will free of the thought-emotion-thought vicious cycle. Then you are able to use simple logic. Then, you will realize that right now, you have a job. If and when you lose the job, you may be able to find another job, sooner or later. In the meantime, simplify your living: distinguish between true

193

necessities of life versus your lifestyle. Save some money, which will come handy when you don't have a job.

Q: Isn't fear good for us? It helps us to survive.

A: There is a myth that *"it's natural to have fear. It may even be good for us. It helps us to survive."* From the perspective of your Acquired Self, it is a perfect statement. Since a most people are in the grip of their Acquired Self, this kind of statement seems quite reasonable to them.

Let's take a close look at this concept using simple logic.

What happens when you are faced with a threat? Let's say you're walking through a forest and suddenly, you're face to face with a bear. You take immediate action *without thinking*. There is no time for thinking. Instantaneously, you either *fight* or *run away*. This intelligence resides in your body. It prepares you instantaneously by releasing a large amount of adrenaline in the blood stream, which raises your heart rate, blood pressure and blood glucose enabling you to deal with the situation immediately. You are physically *primed* to fight or run away. This is the so-called *Fight or Flight* response, which happens instantaneously, once you are faced with a real threat. With your immediate action, you will either survive or die. <u>So far there is no fear</u>.

Let's presume you survived the situation. A few moments later, you start thinking, *"What could have happened? I could have died or lost a leg and be paralyzed for the rest of my life. If I had died, what would have happened to my wife and kids?."* Now intense fear sets in.

At the time of the actual threatening situation, there was no fear, but thinking about it creates fear.

It's the action at the time of the threatening situation that saves your life. So it is not fear, but your spontaneous action in a situation that may save your life.

Fear Actually Harms Your Body

The entire experience of facing the bear and your conditioned mind's *interpretation and reaction* gets stored in your memory box and becomes added to your Acquired Self.

Let's say a month later, you tell your story to a friend. It is basically your memory box repeating the stored event. Even though there is no bear in front of you, your conditioned mind sees a bear and warns your body of this virtual threat. Obviously, there is a big difference between the real bear and the virtual bear. *However, your body cannot distinguish between a real and virtual threat. It relies on your mind.* So if your mind sees a threat, so does your body. Therefore, your body responds to this virtual threat the same way as it did to the real threat: by releasing adrenaline. Your heart starts pounding, blood pressure rises and blood glucose rises. In addition, you also think, "what might have happened" and this thinking creates a lot of fear. The net result: you have an unpleasant sensation of fear and physical symptoms of your heart pounding, a rise in blood pressure and blood sugar. Of course, your friends also join in with various thoughts of, "what could have happened." They may tell you about a similar story they saw on TV or read in the newspaper. From these collective thoughts, you all build up a cloud of fear.

Now here is another interesting fact: **Since you can neither fight nor flee this virtual situation, the situation does not resolve.** Your body continues to release adrenaline as long as your memory (part of your Acquired Self) and your friends' stories continue to generate the virtual threat. You continue to experience fear and its damaging effects on the body as long as you have fearful thoughts. There is no resolution of the situation.

After tormenting you for a while, your Acquired Self (your memory and thoughts) settles back down in the memory box, ready to be awakened each time you talk or think about your deadly experience.

Fear not only causes Anxiety, Insomnia, Panic attacks and Phobias but also leads to High Blood Pressure, Diabetes, Heart Attacks and Autoimmune Diseases. For details please, refer to my book, "Stress Cure Now."

Q: I suffer from chronic pain. I have seen several doctors, but there is nothing they can do. I get so frustrated. Why Me? I am a good person at heart, but I cannot enjoy life. It is not fair.

A: You suffer from a chronic pain. There are two components to it: physical pain and Psychological pain.

Let us first look at the psychological pain, which adds to your physical pain. The emotions of frustration, anger and unfairness cause you to have psychological pain, which adds to your physical pain. Additionally, your REAL Self is stained by these emotions. In this way, your load of "emotional stains" continues to get heavier and heavier.

Who is this "I" who gets frustrated, who feels a victim of unfairness? It is your Acquired Self. Based on the "book of role description," you judge yourself to be a good person. This book gives rise to expectations: "If you are a good person, then life should be good to you." Instead, life gave you chronic pain. Obviously, your Acquired Self is annoyed, frustrated and angry at this unfairness.

Once you are free of your Acquired Self and the Collective Acquired Self of the Society, you realize the book of role description is simply a description, written by society, not by life. It is your society's collective Acquired Self that made you the promise of fairness, not the REAL life.

Your Acquired Self is virtual, unreal. But it triggers emotions, which are real and are felt by your REAL Self, who gets tarnished. One day, your REAL Self will leave your physical body, upon your death. But, by then, it would have accumulated a huge load of emotional stains, and will continue to suffer from the emotional pains, even after the death of your body.

Once you realize that the Acquired Self is *not* you at all, it is simply a tool to function in society and once you are *not* stuck to your Acquired Self, you do *not* believe in the book of role description any longer, then expectations automatically vanish. That's how you stop adding more emotional pains to you – your REAL Self.

Keep shifting attention away from your thoughts, and into the REAL NOW in front of your eyes: what you see, hear, smell, taste and touch, as well as the space, silence and stillness. Once you live like this, even the physical pain may lessen in its intensity.

Dr. Zaidi's Quotes

- Keep your mind where your body is.

- Your conditioned, busy mind is the root cause of your stress. You are not born with this. You acquire it from your society as you grow up.

- The past and future are mental abstractions, virtual and unreal. The present moment is the only *real* thing. Live in it if you want to live a *real* life.

- Many people live a conditional life. In their minds, certain conditions have to be met before they will start living their life. That day never arrives, because they keep adding more and more conditions and goals.

- Excessive thinking about the future is the major reason for fear, anxiety and panic attacks.

- You can only solve a problem if it exists, but your busy mind creates a virtual problem and then it tries to take care of this phantom. How absurd!

- Frustrations arise from expectations, which originate from your conditioned mind.

- Most human interactions are actually based upon "conditioned minds interacting." That's why there is so much stress in our lives.

- You can be free of your conditioned mind simply by observing it in action. Don't hate it or you will make it stronger. Simply observing it is enough.

- Human problems can only be solved by humans.

- Live in your field of awareness, created by your five senses: what you see, hear, taste, smell and touch. If it is not in your field of awareness, it is unreal for you at that moment.

- Keep asking yourself two questions: "Is it happening right now, at this very moment, in my field of awareness?" and "What is happening right now in my field of awareness?"

- True living is like watching a movie, playing continuously around you and realizing that you are also in the movie.

- Concepts divide human beings and that is the basis of conflict and violence. True freedom from violence lies in freedom from concepts.

- Concept is not reality and reality is not conceptual.

- We all live in a conceptual world and mistakenly take it for real.

- REAL GOD is all around you and inside you. It cannot be described because language itself is conceptual.

- Age is a concept.

- The source of stress as well as joy lies inside you.

- Make the ultimate choice to be stress-free without any outside help.

- Logic is the ultimate asset we humans have.

- Get rid of the filters created by your conditioned mind. Then, take a fresh look at your life with the lightning rod of *logic.*

- Free yourself from the Virtual Self in order to be stress-free in this life and the life after death.

Acknowledgements

First of all, I deeply acknowledge Lisa, Dorothy, Susan, Julie, Pardeep and my brother for sharing their extraordinary experiences with me and the readers of this book.

I am sincerely grateful to Dolly Najla Zaidi for doing an excellent job proofreading this book.

I also want to express my gratitude to my wife, Georgie, for being my partner in this virtual world, and our daughter, Zareena, for being a wise person at her young age.

About Dr. Sarfraz Zaidi, MD

Dr. Sarfraz Zaidi, MD, is a leading Endocrinologist in the U.S.A. He is a medical expert on thyroid, diabetes, vitamin D, and stress management. He is the director of the Jamila Diabetes and Endocrine Medical Center in Thousand Oaks, California. He is a former assistant Clinical Professor of Medicine at UCLA.

Books and Articles:

Dr. Zaidi is the author of these books:**"Reverse Your Type 2 Diabetes Scientifically", "Power of Vitamin D", "Stress Cure Now", Graves' Disease And Hyperthyroidism", Hypothyroidism And Hashimoto's Thyroiditis", "Stress Management for Teenagers, Parents and Teenagers", "Take Charge of Your Diabetes".** In addition, he has authored numerous articles in prestigious medical journals.

Memberships:

Dr. Zaidi is a Member of the American Association of Clinical Endocrinologists (AACE). In 1997, Dr. Zaidi was inducted as a Fellow to the American College of Physicians (FACP). In 1999, he was honored to be a Fellow of the American College of Endocrinology (FACE).

Speaker:

Dr. Zaidi has been a guest speaker at medical conferences and also frequently lectures the public. He has been interviewed on TV, newspapers and national magazines. Dr. Zaidi is the former director of the Endocrine Clinic at the Olive-View UCLA Medical Center where he taught resident physicians undergoing training in Diabetes and Endocrinology.

Internet:

Dr. Zaidi also regularly writes on these websites:

205

www.OnlineMedinfo, which provides in depth knowledge about endocrine disorders such as, Thyroid, Parathyroid, Vitamin D Osteoporosis, Obesity, PreDiabetes, Metabolic Syndrome, Menopause, Low Testosterone, Adrenal, Pituitary and More.
www.DiabetesSpecialist, which is dedicated to providing extensive knowledge to Diabetics.
www.InnerPeaceAndLove, which is an inspirational website, exploring the Mind-Body connection.
He regularly writes on his Blog.
www.onlinemedinfo.com/blog/
He has done educational YouTube videos about Vitamin D
www.youtube.com/user/georgie6988
And about Insulin resistance, diabetes and heart disease.
www.youtube.com/user/TheDiabetesEducation?feature=guide
His main website: www.DoctorZaidi.com

Other Books by Dr. Sarfraz Zaidi, MD

Stress Cure Now

In his groundbreaking book, Dr. Zaidi describes a truly *New* approach to deal with stress.

Dr. Zaidi's strategy to cure stress is based on his personal awakening, in-depth medical knowledge and vast clinical experience. It is simple, direct, original and therefore, profound. He uses logic - the common sense that every human is born with.

Using the torch of logic, Dr. Zaidi shows you that the true root cause of stress actually resides inside you, not out there. Therefore, the solution must also reside inside you.

In **"Stress Cure Now,"** Dr. Zaidi guides you to see the true root cause of your stress, in its deepest layers. Only then you can get rid of it from its roots, once and for all.

Stress Management For Teenagers, Parents And Teachers

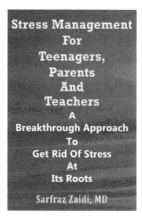

Using the blazing torch of logic, Dr. Zaidi cuts through the stress triangle of teenagers, parents and teachers.

This original, profound and breakthrough approach is completely different from the usual, customary approaches to manage stress, which simply work as a band-aid, while the volcano underneath continues to smolder. Sooner or later, it erupts through the paper- thin layers of these superficial strategies.

Dr. Zaidi guides you step by step on how you can be free of various forms of stress. From peer pressure, to stress from education, to conflict between teenagers, parents and teachers, to anxiety, addictions and ADD, Dr. Zaidi covers every aspect of stress teenagers, parents and teachers experience in their day-to-day life. Dr. Zaidi's new approach ushers in a new era in psychology, yet this book is such an easy read. It's like talking to a close friend for practical, useful yet honest advice that works.

Power of Vitamin D

"Power of Vitamin D," has become a popular and a reference book on the topic of vitamin D. This book contains all the important information you need to know about Vitamin D including the wonderful health benefits of Vitamin D.

In this book, Dr. Zaidi dispels common myths about Vitamin D, such as "being outdoor in the sun for 15 minutes a day is enough to take care of your Vitamin D needs." Wrong!

Most people are low in Vitamin D and they don't even know it! Sadly, most physicians are not up-to-date on Vitamin D. They often order the wrong test for Vitamin D level, which can be normal even if you have a severe deficiency of Vitamin D!

Many physicians interpret test results of Vitamin D with the myopic eye of the reference range provided by the laboratory. These reference ranges are often wrong when it comes to Vitamin D. Dr. Zaidi explains how you can achieve the optimal level of Vitamin in order to take advantage of the miraculous heath benefits of Vitamin D, without risking its toxicity.

Hypothyroidism And Hashimoto's Thyroiditis

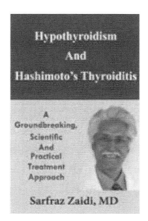

The current treatment of Hypothyroidism is superficial and unsatisfactory. Patients continue to suffer from the symptoms of Hypothyroidism, despite taking thyroid pills. Even worse, there is no treatment for Hashimoto's Thyroiditis, the root cause of hypothyroidism in a large number of patients.

Dr. Sarfraz Zaidi, MD, has made a breakthrough discovery about the real cause of Hashimoto's Thyroiditis, and how to effectively treat it. He has also made new insights into the causes of Hypothyroidism. Based on these groundbreaking discoveries, he has developed a revolutionary approach to treat Hypothyroidism and cure Hashimoto's Thyroiditis.

In "Hypothyroidism And Hashimoto's Thyroiditis, A Breakthrough Approach to Effective Treatment," you will find out.

- Why you continue to suffer from symptoms of Hypothyroidism, despite taking thyroid pills?
- What really is Hypothyroidism?
- What are the symptoms of Hypothyroidism?
- Why the diagnosis of Hypothyroidism is often missed?

- Why the current treatment approach of hypothyroidism is unscientific?
- Why the usual tests for thyroid function are inaccurate and misleading?
- What actually causes Hypothyroidism?
- What is the root cause of Hashimoto's Thyroiditis, besides genetics?
- What other conditions are commonly associated with Hashimoto's Thyroiditis?
- How to effectively treat Hypothyroidism?
- How to cure Hashimoto's Thyroiditis?
- And a detailed thyroid diet that works.

Graves' Disease And Hyperthyroidism

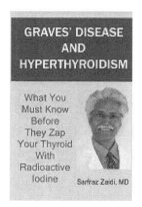

Graves' disease is one of several causes of hyperthyroidism.

In "Graves' Disease And Hyperthyroidism", Dr. Zaidi, describes how to accurately diagnose and treat Graves' disease as well as other causes of hyperthyroidism.

The medical treatment of Graves' disease has not changed in over 50 years. Sad, but true! The standard, usual treatment with radioactive iodine is a superficial, myopic approach. It almost always makes you hypothyroid (underactive thyroid state). Then, you need to be on thyroid pills for the rest of your life. In addition, radioactive iodine does not treat the underlying root cause of Graves' disease - autoimmune dysfunction, which continues to smolder and easily erupts into another autoimmune disease. Anti-thyroid drugs do not treat autoimmune dysfunction either. They provide only temporary relief. Often, symptoms return once you stop these drugs. Surgery also does not treat autoimmune dysfunction. It often leads to hypothyroidism as well as many other complications.

Over the last ten years, Dr. Zaidi developed a truly breakthrough approach to get rid of Graves' disease at its roots - autoimmune dysfunction. His patients have benefited tremendously from this approach. Now is the time for you to learn about this groundbreaking discovery.

Dr. Zaidi reveals what really causes autoimmune dysfunction that ultimately leads to Graves' disease. His revolutionary treatment strategy consists of five components: His unique Diet for Graves' disease (including original recipes), the link between Vitamin D deficiency and Graves' disease, the connection between Graves' disease and Vitamin B12 deficiency, how Stress causes Graves' disease (and Dr. Zaidi's unique strategy to manage stress) and the Judicious use of Anti-Thyroid drugs.

Reverse Your Type 2 Diabetes Scientifically

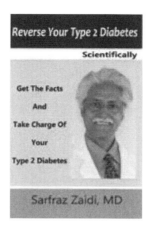

There is a common misconception among patients as well physicians that treating Type 2 diabetes means controlling your blood sugar by any means. This approach is dangerously flawed. The fact is that Type 2 diabetes is a complex disease process. If not managed properly, it often leads to a number of horrendous complications. Sometimes, medications can cause more harm than good.

In "Reverse Your Type 2 Diabetes Scientifically," Dr. Sarfraz Zaidi, MD explains what is the root cause of Type 2 diabetes. Then he showcases his unique 5-step approach to manage this disease at its roots. Over the last fifteen years, he has employed this groundbreaking approach to help thousands of Type 2 diabetic patients. He has included actual case studies from his clinical practice to illustrate how his 5-step approach can reverse Type 2 diabetes as well as its complications.

Dr. Zaidi's unique 5-step approach consists of:

1. A simple, yet profound approach to Stress Management, based on his personal awakening.

2. A revolutionary, scientific approach to diet. You may be surprised to learn how Calorie-based dietary recommendations are actually *not* very scientific. His diet is based on actual food items you buy in your grocery store or farmers market. He has included 75 of his own recipes. He also gives you a practical guide to eat at home or eat-out at various ethnic restaurants.

3. A new, scientific approach to exercise. You may be surprised to learn how too much exercise can actually be quite harmful.

4. An in-depth, scientific description of vitamins, minerals and herbs that are valuable in managing Type 2 diabetes.

5. Prescription medications, when necessary. A comprehensive description about: How various medications work, what are the advantages, disadvantages and side-effects of each drug.

All books available at major online retailers.

http://www.DoctorZaidi.com

Made in the USA
San Bernardino, CA
14 January 2015